Your Child Is * Smarter * Than You Think

Your Child Is *Smarter* Than You Think

Peggy Eastman
with John L. Barr, M.D.

WILLIAM MORROW AND COMPANY, INC.
New York

Copyright © 1985 by Peggy Eastman and John L. Barr, M.D.

Grateful acknowledgment is made to the following photographers and agencies for the photographs in this book:

Chapter 1: Carl J. Pfeifer/N.C. News Service
Chapter 2: Vivienne della Grotta
Chapter 3: Charles A. Blahusch/N.C. News Service
Chapter 4: Vivienne della Grotta
Chapter 5: Jim Frost/N.C. News Service
Chapter 6: Kati Ritchie/N.C. News Service
Chapter 7: Dale G. Folstad/N.C. News Service
Chapter 8: Frank Methe/N.C. News Service
Chapter 9: Richard C. Finke/N.C. News Service
Chapter 10: Dave Breen/N.C. News Service
Chapter 11: Jim Kilcoyne/N.C. News Service
Chapter 12: Tom Kane/N.C. News Service

A portion of Chapter Three appeared in *Self* magazine.

All rights reserved. No part of this book may be reproduced or utilized in any form or by any means, electronic or mechanical, including photocopying, recording or by any information storage and retrieval system, without permission in writing from the Publisher. Inquiries should be addressed to Permissions Department, William Morrow and Company, Inc., 105 Madison Ave., New York, N.Y. 10016.

Library of Congress Cataloging in Publication Data

Eastman, Peggy.
    Your child is smarter than you think.

    Bibliography: p.
    Includes index.
    1. Child development.   2. Learning, Psychology of.
I. Barr, John L.   II. Title.
HQ767.9.E255   1985   155.4'13   84-19086
ISBN 0-688-02965-5

Printed in the United States of America

First Edition

1 2 3 4 5 6 7 8 9 10

BOOK DESIGN BY ELLEN LO GIUDICE

For Christopher and Alice—
if the world would only believe what
nature shows us through children

Acknowledgments

No book springs into being full-blown. Just as a baby takes a long gestation period, so there is a long gestation period for any book. For helping with this important process, we are deeply indebted to Isabelle O. Barr and Bulah C. Eastman, who have dedicated their lives to helping young children learn. We are grateful to all the researchers whose creative and meticulous work has elevated the study of child development to a science. We are grateful to teachers in many disciplines—physiology, psychology, psychiatry, literature—who stimulated in us a deep respect for the learning process. For help in pulling information together, we are especially grateful to Tineke Boddé Haase of the National Institute of Child Health and Human Development, Judith Folkenberg of the National Institute of Mental Health, Emily Schrag of the National Center for Clinical Infant Programs, and Janet Brown of the National Association for the Education of Young Children.

Preface

Your child is a genius.

Your child is a genius in the sense that his or her capacity for learning is virtually limitless. Your baby comes into the world with brand-new skin, wiggly fingers and toes, and a brain primed for learning. Everything he sees, hears, touches, and tastes is an adventure. Your baby's appealing cooing and gurgling and purposeful crawling, reaching, and grasping are efforts at learning. How well your child learns starting from birth will help to determine how well your child will use his unique abilities and gifts, and the kind of contribution he will make to this world.

Before your child reaches the age of three, he will have most of the basic mental tools he will need for a lifetime of learning. He will have learned about cause and effect, spatial relations, language, and motion. He will have developed memory skills and the ability to concentrate. He will have developed a sense of self-worth and mastery—essential to effective learning.

You are your child's first and most important teacher. During the early years, your encouragement and efforts to create learning experiences for your child are crucial to his or her development. Many of these things you probably do anyway, without even thinking about them. You don't need flash cards (the crutches of adult learning) and you shouldn't try to teach your preschool child formal tasks such as reading and writing. That comes later.

Preface

This book was written for the parents of children between the ages of one day and five years. Up until about the age of five, children are in a stage known as "preoperational," a stage when learning comes through doing. Effective learning at this stage isn't the kind of learning that has to do with forming letters to write your name. It isn't trying to memorize pictures or words. It isn't what we adults think of as learning: sitting at a desk and doing what the teacher says. Your child's early exposure to his kind of learning—on his own level—will have a lot to do with how much he learns to love the process of formal education later.

Early learning is exploring, trying things out, putting sounds together to make words. It's having fun with puzzles and blocks. It's climbing a jungle gym or sitting quietly turning the pages of a cloth picture book. It's pre-education, in the sense that this important exploring period precedes formal schooling.

In the last twenty years, an impressive and growing body of research has focused on the importance of early learning. It wasn't so very long ago that newborns were considered to be helpless little creatures who couldn't see, hear, or communicate. We now know that a healthy newborn is a competent individual who can not only see and hear, but has a definite personality and is capable of making his or her wishes known by facial expressions, gestures, and sounds.

New excitement about the value of stimulating the intellectual as well as the physical development of even very young children is grounded in the realization that intelligence is malleable, not fixed. While part of a child's potential is determined by his or her genes—powers and inclinations inherited from parents—that is only part of the story.

Preface

Geniuses may indeed be born, but they can also be made or unmade. Little intellectual stars do not just naturally perform with minimal training or effort. Instead, although many so-called child prodigies have the innate ability to become stars in their chosen fields, they never realize that stardom without a tremendous amount of practice and specific training, and a great deal of caring, loving direction.

There are those who say that we don't really know enough yet about how babies and young children learn to be able to translate research findings into practical guidelines for parent-teachers. We don't agree. Our children are too valuable a resource for us not to try to make use of the important findings now emerging from child development research.

It's true that babies and preschoolers can't tell us exactly how they learn. We must rely on the observations of researchers in such diverse fields as education, psychology, medicine, and the creative arts. But we know they start learning from the very moment they're born. If you have a newborn at home, you've probably already noticed that although the baby spends a lot of time sleeping, he or she is also surprisingly observant and responsive. Even a tiny newborn responds to sounds in the range of human speech. As early as the first day after birth, many newborns will move their tiny bodies in harmony with the cadence of human voices.

You've probably also noticed that your infant is fascinated by the human face. A baby even as young as two and one-half months will look at a smiling human face and respond by smiling repeatedly, taking natural delight in face-to-face contact. You don't need to be told your smiling child is a responsive learner; you already know it.

The point of this book is to help you become more at-

Preface

tuned to your child's unique mental potential and natural creativity. Just as you often know your baby is sick before your pediatrician does, so you are most qualified to provide your baby with the loving stimulation that will allow him or her to grow into a unique person with independence, stamina, curiosity, and a special way of sharing innate gifts with the world.

There are important reasons for parents to try to give their children valuable early learning experiences in a natural, unforced way. Recent studies on our public education system have revealed a bleak picture of children graduating from high school who cannot read, write, or reason. One of the direst of these reports, written by the National Commission on Excellence in Education, is called "A Nation at Risk," and is billed as "An Open Letter to the American People."

The report reveals that fully 13 percent of all seventeen-year-olds in the United States are illiterate, and that the scores of high-school students on most standardized tests are lower than they were some twenty years ago. The commission report charges that the educational underpinnings of our society are "being eroded by a rising tide of mediocrity that threatens our very future as a Nation and a people." Strong words for a strong charge. The report goes on to list sweeping recommendations to reform our "mediocre" educational system.

We believe that the importance of this report is not so much what it says about secondary education—although that is certainly shocking and demands remedies—but what it says to parents about nurturing a philosophy of learning in babies and preschoolers. "As surely as you are your child's first and most influential teacher, your child's ideas about education and its significance begin with you," says the report, addressing itself directly to parents.

Preface

Think about it. A baby who is not encouraged to explore and learn on her own level will become turned off to learning. She may come to feel there's something wrong with her curiosity and her natural gropings to understand her world better. She may start to behave like unloved, unstimulated children who lie listlessly in their cribs, waiting for others to do things for them.

When children whose natural curiosity has not been cherished and encouraged enter school, reading and writing become boring chores, not adventures of the mind. No wonder such children graduate without knowing how to read, write, or reason. Undoubtedly their natural creativity, sense of wonder, and natural desire to learn were not nurtured. Chances are that the lack of nurturing started very early—at home. It's a rare teacher, no matter how gifted, who can make up for five years of neglect at home.

It's your child; the right way to raise your baby is the way you choose to do it. There is no magic blueprint that can guarantee your baby success in later years. But if you instill a sense of excitement about learning in your child and give him or her a sense of successful accomplishment and performance, those qualities will last.

This book was written for the parents of healthy children with normal intelligence. It wasn't written for the parents of children with physical problems or learning disabilities. Those are the topics for other, equally important books. In ours you will learn the scientific basis for helping your child learn; how to make your home a creative environment in which to raise a child; how to help your child learn through his senses; how to use the important tools of myth and fantasy in storytelling to draw out your child's natural creativity; how to help your developing child experience the feeling of success and mastery; and how to

Preface

help your child develop thought patterns that will help his or her body stay well.

Remember, no one will ever be as influential as you in shaping your child's attitude toward learning. How you use that influence is entirely up to you. If this book helps you to realize that your child is, in fact, a genius when it comes to his or her capacity to learn, and that you are your child's most important teacher, then it will have served its purpose.

—P. E. and J. L. B.
Washington, D.C., May 1984

Contents

Acknowledgments
Preface
1 • Early Learning: Why All the Fuss?   17
2 • Superbabies: Born to Learn   41
3 • The Senses: Doors to Learning   63
4 • Stimulation: How Much, How Often, What Kind?   87
5 • More Than Child's Play   105
6 • Tell Me a Story   129
7 • Your Home as a Creative School   149
8 • Resilience Begins at Home   177
9 • Making Control Count   195
10 • Beyond Bonding: Fathers Are Parents, Too   217
11 • Early Learning: Where Do We Go from Here?   235
12 • Conclusion: Toward a Learning Society   253
Appendix: Information, Please: Resources for Parents   267
Selected Bibliography   273
Index   281

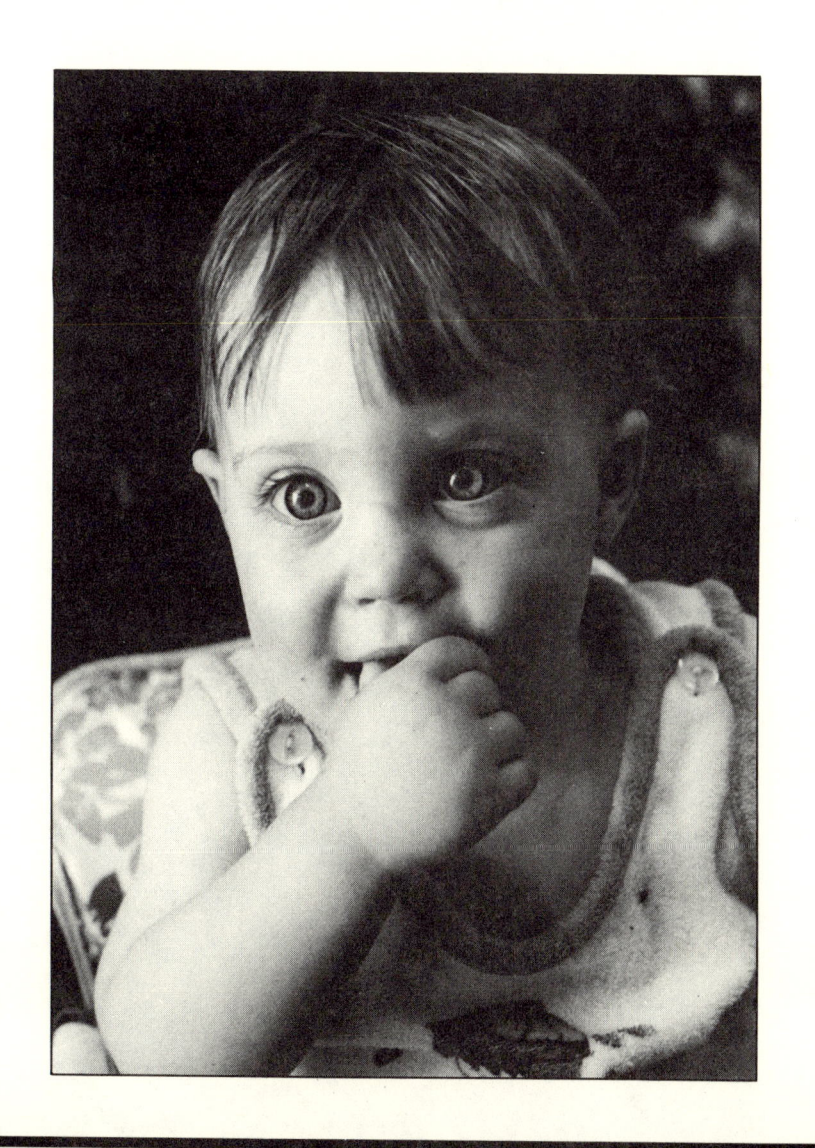

1. Early Learning: Why All the Fuss?

> This learning of the first eighteen months is a prodigious intellectual feat. No wonder every parent thinks his baby is a genius. He is!
>
> —SELMA H. FRAIBERG, *The Magic Years*

For most of the history of childhood, the genius of young children was a well-kept secret. The children themselves knew, but somehow adults weren't getting the message. Only in the last twenty years or so have researchers and educators begun to appreciate what children are capable of learning at early ages, and what parents can do to help that process along.

Sadly, the history of childhood is a wasteland that has ignored children's capacity to learn and need for nurturing. Throughout history, adults have subjected children to physical and sexual abuse, child neglect, and child labor. Certainly there have been wonderful parents down through the ages; but no one really knows how many potential geniuses throughout history have been nonproductive because someone abused them, or failed to give them love, attention, and the experiences of early learning.

Although it seems shocking to us today, adults in earlier centuries regularly tied up infants, bound children in corsets, terrorized them with scare tales of ghostlike figures, left toddlers alone at home for hours, beat them, and—the worst crime—practiced infanticide with babies they didn't want (girls or handicapped infants). Since the eighteenth century, treatment of children has been more humane, as adults have come to realize that children aren't miniature adults but beings with unique needs, capacities, and personalities. It was Sigmund Freud, the father of psychoanalysis, who essentially discovered childhood as a unique world of its own. He found that many of our adult fantasies, anxieties, and irrational thoughts actually stem from early childhood experiences and memories.

Swiss psychologist Jean Piaget then took the next step with direct observation of children, reported in such pioneering books as *The Language and Thought of the Child*. Piaget has had a profound influence on our understanding of how children grow and think. Although his methods would be considered highly unscientific today (he basically just observed his own three children), Piaget's painstaking observations provide an essential framework for studying children. So important is Piaget to child development research that he spawned an entire group of authors who spend their time writing books interpreting Piaget.

Not Just Little Adults

In a scholarly but brutal book detailing some of the abuses of children throughout history, *The History of Childhood*, Lloyd deMause points out that the evolution of childhood has been a "series of closer approaches between adult and child, with each closing of psychic distance producing fresh anxiety." He simply means that the more we've begun to understand our tiny charges, the more anxious and responsible we've become about serving them well. The child-rearing practices of each age have been adapted to reduce that level of anxiety, theorizes DeMause. In general, he found, the further back one goes in history (and the further adults were from understanding children), the more dismal child care was and the less effective parents were in interpreting children's needs.

In many paintings of earlier centuries, the proportion and scale of children are wrong: the eyes should be larger in relation to the head, the heads bigger in relation to the body, and the arms and legs shorter in proportion to the trunk. Basically, adults painted children as little adults: reflecting the thinking that they *were* little adults.

Today we paint children as children, and we treat them as unique individuals with special skills and needs. In a sense, the current interest in stimulating babies and young children to learn is the result of a natural educational process on the part of parents that has evolved over time. Realizing that babies are competent, bright, and responsive is the first step toward deciding to do something about developing all that competence and infant brainpower.

Because of Piaget, we now know that there are basically three stages in a child's intellectual development. The first stage, called the pre-operational stage, is the one we're concerned with in this book. This is the preschool stage, the one that ends roughly at the age of five. In this pre-operational stage, your child is working to establish cause-and-effect relationships, mostly by manipulating his environment through action. He shakes a rattle and gets a sound; crawls to reach a ball on the floor; piles blocks one on top of the other and then, with a swipe of his hand, tumbles them to the floor.

During this stage of growth, your child isn't really able to separate his own goals from the real world. He wants food: he cries or reaches toward the cracker box and says "Cracker." He doesn't want the cracker in five minutes, he wants it *now*. He can't begin to understand why the world doesn't always meet his needs. Pre-operational children aren't able to wait while adults talk to each other; they'll butt in and make their wishes known. Since your child can't really separate his own world from the larger world, his reality may in fact appear quite selfish to you.

Piaget's two later stages of development are called the stage of concrete operations and the stage of formal operations. An operation in this sense is simply a means of getting information about the real world into the mind and there transforming that information so it can be used to solve problems. Elementary-school children can carry out concrete operations. A formal operation is a slightly more complicated mental procedure; somewhere between the ages of ten and fourteen your child will learn to form a hypothesis—a theory that something is true—based on the knowledge she has gained about the world. That ability to form a hypothesis is a formal operation in Piaget's sense.

The Wire Monkey

In addition to Piaget, a number of other scientists have made important contributions to our understanding of how babies develop and what they need. In the 1940s, a scientist named Harry Harlow began to study how mother monkeys care for their babies during the first months of life. Harlow noted that when baby monkeys were separated from their mothers very early, the babies became withdrawn and unhappy, even though they were physically healthy and had plenty to eat. He found that a pretend mother made of wire, covered with soft cloth, and equipped with a bottle served as a mother substitute for baby monkeys. They preferred the soft cloth "mother" to a mechanical wire one that was not soft.

When Harlow put baby monkeys in total isolation, where they had no contact with other monkeys or humans, they

Early Learning: Why All the Fuss?

became antisocial, huddling in their cages. Later exposure to other monkeys didn't help; they remained antisocial. And when some of these monkeys later had babies of their own, they ignored them or struck them. Monkeys who had never been mothered didn't know how to be good mothers.

Monkeys aren't humans, of course, and not all Harlow's observations can be categorically applied to people. But two other scientists observed similar results in human babies. René Spitz studied children in a Latin American orphanage who, while they were getting all the food they needed, weren't getting enough human attention because the orphanage was short-staffed. What Spitz found was that if a child didn't get constant, loving attention from one human being, the child often didn't develop normally—a syndrome doctors call "failure to thrive." Despite plenty of food, the babies got sick often and became apathetic and uninterested in everything around them.

In England, psychiatrist John Bowlby carefully observed how babies and mothers interact with each other in the early months. He concluded that a baby's behavior is specifically designed to "win over" a particular adult—usually Mother—to his or her charms. The adult, completely smitten, becomes attuned to the baby's needs and can almost anticipate them. Bowlby called this process of special closeness between baby and adult "attachment," and concluded that attachment is vital to an infant's sense of competence, confidence, and curiosity about the world.

Physicians John Kennell and Marshall Klaus took the concept of attachment one step further. They said that an infant needs to "bond" to the parent as soon after birth as possible—preferably within minutes. Early bonding also helps parents, biologically motivating them to the responsibility of nurturing their offspring. In pioneering work at Case Western Reserve Hospital in Cleveland, they promoted bonding, even with premature babies. They encouraged contact between parents and premature babies, even when the parents had to reach through an incubator to touch their children.

Some critics feel that the concept of bonding has been overvalued, that it has been interpreted as a "magic moment" after birth which, if missed, is detrimental to a child. Certainly adoptive parents are able to achieve just as much closeness with their babies as parents who had the experience of bonding directly after birth. But Kennell and Klaus's bonding studies have had a healthy and significant effect on hospital practices; no longer are normal, healthy infants swooped away from their healthy mothers after birth and taken to nurseries to lie anonymously with other babies where their parents can't touch them, feed them, or hold them.

The Bonding Boon: Humanizing Hospitals

Studies on bonding and attachment have affected other practices in delivery rooms and newborn nurseries, too. Fathers are now encouraged to be present during delivery in most hospitals, and some hospitals encourage fathers to stay even when the birth must be done by cesarean section. Nurses are encouraged to provide stimulation and love for babies as well as physical care, especially for babies who are not thriving and developing well. They use toys that encourage the babies to reach, pictures to encourage them to focus their eyes, and records with music to stimulate their sense of hearing. They stroke the babies to give them a sense of their own bodies and comfort them.

Nurses and nurse-educators have started infant stimulation programs for babies in newborn nurseries, pro-

Early Learning: Why All the Fuss?

grams designed to help them focus their eyes, learn to grasp objects, discriminate shapes, and react to human speech. Kathryn M. Barnard, a nurse-educator at the University of Washington, has led the way in identifying and helping babies who are at high risk of mental problems, while Susan M. Ludington, a certified nurse-midwife, University of California (Los Angeles) teacher, and founder of the Infant Stimulation Education Association, has pioneered the infant stimulation movement among nurses in hospital nurseries.

Some hospitals have extended their work to older babies and started programs designed to help children who appear to be at risk for emotional or mental problems. For instance, the Primary Intervention Program (nicknamed "PIP") at the Convalescent Hospital for Children in Rochester, New York, is aimed at identifying and providing special help to at-risk children between the ages of six and thirty-six months. A therapist regularly visits the homes of babies and young children who are showing signs of emotional problems (such as hyperactivity or depression) and works with parents for thirty minutes at a time to help them know how to help their children with words, toys, and games. Robert S. Lustig, the staff psychologist who coordinates the PIP program, believes that such programs are important because they reach children *early*—before destructive behavior begins.

A second program at Convalescent Hospital for Children is aimed at facing and diluting the quite natural stress many new parents feel after the birth of their babies. Kathleen Gilliam, a social worker who serves as director of outpatient services at the hospital, notes that feelings of ambivalence about a new baby, though quite normal, aren't accepted by the public. Parents aren't supposed to feel doubts or concerns—just joy. The hospital's Postpartum

Project, a group program that meets weekly, helps new parents to share their fears and ambivalence and to learn how to help their babies.

In recent years, helping new parents and helping children earlier have become major themes among professionals who work with young children. Along with the increasing recognition of a baby's marvelous capacities has come the realization that things that are going wrong can be set straight if parents and babies are reached early. Pediatrician T. Berry Brazelton, child psychologist Burton L. White, and psychiatrist Stanley I. Greenspan are among the professionals who have emphasized the need to start working with children from birth—not when they are three, four, five, or six.

"Three is too late" has become a shared theme among professionals who care about children. The nonprofit National Center for Clinical Infant Programs, headquartered in Washington, D.C., is one of the important national groups focusing attention on providing professional help to infants who need it, when they need it.

"In order to produce a nation of healthy, competent children, education must begin in the earliest months and years of life, when the nervous system is growing most rapidly," is the view of Greenspan, a National Institute of Mental Health clinical infant researcher who is one of the driving forces behind the National Center. He feels it is now possible to detect emotional problems in infants as young as two months old—and certainly within the first two years of life. Until recently, severe emotional disturbances in babies went undetected until the children had reached school; by then, destructive emotional patterns had already been set.

Early Learning: Why All the Fuss?

Infants Under Investigation

Can scientists really learn much about babies from studying babies? After all, they can't talk, walk, or do much for themselves. But the answer is a resounding yes. Infants can be studied and much can be learned from and about them. The weighty, nearly five-hundred-page book of abbreviated presentations for a recent meeting of the Society for Research in Child Development reflects how far scientists have come in understanding babies and young children. Here is just a smattering of the titles of presentations made by researchers at the meeting:

- "Individual Variation in Mother–Infant Interaction" (Clark University, Worcester, Massachusetts)
- "Sentence Imitation: Can Children Remember More if They Process in Greater Depth?" (York University, Toronto, Canada)
- "Young Children's Play and Work Activities in Two Cultures" (University of Wisconsin, Madison)
- "Maternal Emotional Signaling and Infants' Reaction to Strangers" (University of Denver)
- "Analyses of Infant Free Play in Naturalistic and Structured Settings" (University of Vermont)
- "Impact of Neonatal Temperament on Caregiver Behavior" (University of North Carolina)
- "Parents' Identification of Their Infants on the Basis of Cries" (Northern Illinois University)
- "Perception of Three-Dimensional Form in Infancy" (Swarthmore College)

At this meeting, which was held in Detroit, child development researchers cut a broad swath in their discussions. They examined everything from what makes babies kick to how children play symbolically to whether babies turn their heads toward brief sounds to how babies too young to speak classify the objects they see.

The point is that child development experts have begun studying children who are significantly younger than those studied in the past. It is now considered perfectly acceptable—indeed, scientific—to stick your tongue out repeatedly at a tiny baby to see whether he will stick his tongue out at you, or to study a baby's cries to see whether you can distinguish a "hungry cry" from a "wet cry" from a "hug me" cry. Researchers, along with educators and parents, have become smitten by the wondrous capabilities of the newborn.

Considering the fact that a child will learn more, faster, before the age of three than he or she ever will again, formal school begins relatively late in a youngster's life. A child is generally five by the time he goes to kindergarten, six by the time he gets to first grade. What this means is not that children should start school earlier (they shouldn't) but that parents are their children's first and by far the most important teachers. What it also means is that your home is your child's first and most important school.

It may sound like an awesome responsibility—"Along with the feeding and changing and loving I have to teach, too?"—but the fact is, your child is such a natural learner that the whole concept of teaching becomes fun, natural, and easy. We are not talking about schoolroom teaching, which is largely based on memorization of facts, but on discoveries of the natural world you help your child make for himself.

There is a vast difference between describing objects as your child sees them simply and clearly while you point to them and sitting your child down in front of a flash card that says *cow* or *dog* or *house*. In the first instance you're teaching by following the child's lead—his natural curiosity about what he sees around him—describing what the child can see for himself. In the second instance you're teaching by rote memory.

Rote learning isn't really learning at all: it's memorizing a set of facts. Real learning is not only acquiring new knowledge but determining how to categorize that knowledge and where it fits in relationship to other pieces of knowledge. Real learning involves thinking.

Harvard at One

Unfortunately, new knowledge about the capabilities of young children has produced a syndrome that might best be called the "Harvard at one" syndrome. The relatively recent realization that young children are terrific learners has turned on a light bulb inside some parents' heads. Concerned about doing right by their children, they frantically enroll in expensive courses that purport to teach them how to make their children smarter, subject their children to word flash cards in an effort to teach them to read before kindergarten, and try to push their children into the "best" preschools as if they were vying for Harvard.

It is certainly true that we are finding out young children can learn more, earlier, than we ever thought they could. The catch is that your child must first be ready to learn. This is the "growth readiness" view of mental development, and what it means is simply that certain biological growth steps in your baby's brain must take place before the child is ready, say, to read, spell, write his name, or do mathematical problems.

When a child is "growth ready," these schoolroom kinds of learning experiences will have far more meaning. When her brain cells and eye muscles aren't quite ready to read, trying to teach reading will be frustrating and futile.

One of the most highly publicized of the courses that purport to help parents make their children smarter is given by physical therapist Glenn Doman, founder of the Institutes for the Achievement of Human Potential in Philadelphia. One of these establishments is known as the Better Baby Institute. Doman originally worked with brain-damaged children, then broadened his work to normal children. His treatment method, known as the Doman–Delacato treatment (after C. H. Delacato), makes claims for learning based on "patterning" of the brain. Basically, Doman believes a handicapped child can be helped to learn by being taken back to earlier stages of motor development, such as crawling, where skills are retained, and then working up to more difficult tasks. No one doubts that Doman is a capable individual dedicated to the idea of making children smarter. But the American Academy of Pediatrics (AAP, which represents the nation's pediatricians) has grave reservations about exaggerated claims for the success of his methods, and says so.

In an unusually strongly worded policy statement published in November 1982 in the journal *Pediatrics*, the AAP said: "Claims have been made for a substantial number of cures, and the claims have extended beyond therapy for disease states, asserting that the treatment can make normal children superior, ease world tensions, and possibly 'hasten the evolutionary process.'

"Without supporting data, Doman and Delacato have indicated many typical child rearing practices as limiting a child's potential, thereby increasing the anxiety of already-burdened and confused parents," the AAP continued. The association further said that "Results published

Early Learning: Why All the Fuss?

by or for the Institute have been inconclusive," and "Controlled studies of the Doman–Delacato treatment with respect to reading claims have shown little or no benefit from the treatment."

The association of pediatricians continued: "The Institutes for the Achievement of Human Potential differ substantially from other groups treating developmental problems in 1) the excessive nature of their poorly documented claims for cure and 2) the major demands placed on parents in unswervingly carrying out an unproven technique to the smallest detail." The improvement noted in children following the application of the Doman–Delacato method could simply be based on "the intensive practice of certain isolated skills, or the nonspecific effects of intensive stimulation," the authoritative medical journal noted.

Finally, the AAP warned pediatricians away from the treatment: "Based on past and current analyses, studies, and reports, we must conclude that patterning treatment offers no special merit, that the claims of its advocates are unproven, and that the demands on families are so great that in some cases there may be harm in its use."

Why have we spent all this time discussing an alleged way of making your child smarter? To make the point that you don't need such courses (which may cost as much as five hundred dollars) to tell you how to help your child learn. You don't need the Doman–Delacato method or any other formal "teaching" method to help your normal, bright child become as bright and capable as he or she can be. All you need is an appreciation for how a very young child naturally learns, and an understanding of what you can do at home to help that natural process along.

Mother-Tongue Learning

Did you ever stop and think how a child learns to speak English—or French, or Spanish, or any other native language? The child learns language in a natural, uncontrived, unforced way, by hearing it spoken and by speaking it herself.

One of the soundest, wisest, kindest concepts about how children learn is called the mother-tongue approach, and it comes to us from a Japanese violinist, Shinichi Suzuki. Suzuki, primarily known for his method of teaching tiny children to play the violin (the Suzuki method), believes that the mother-tongue approach to learning—listening and then doing—can be broadened to encompass music and probably other forms of learning as well.

Suzuki, who has developed a following among music instructors and parents in this country, is far from a stern-visaged baton master terrorizing tots into learning how to hold an unfriendly piece of wood under the chin and an errant bow in the hand. What Suzuki argues for is not just producing prodigies who can play the violin at four (his method has been broadened to include the cello and the piano), but something much larger and more significant: an entirely new concept of education that recognizes the innate talents of every child.

President and founder of the Talent Education Institute in Matsumoto, Japan, Suzuki firmly believes that "Talent is no accident of birth," and that all children have the potential of reaching a high intellectual and educational level. In his view—and he is certainly experienced enough by now to know—it's training that builds Beethovens and Mozarts, not just genes. And, he believes, educational training should start from the day of birth, not when a child

Early Learning: Why All the Fuss?

is two or three or five. If a child does not reach his or her full potential, it's the fault of the child's parents and teachers, not the child, argues the Japanese musician.

Suzuki cites an apt example from nature to make his point that talent is trained, not inbred: the nightingale. The nightingale is not born knowing how to sing its exquisite song instinctively. In Japan, nightingales are kept as pet songbirds, much as we keep canaries. In the spring, nightingales that will become pets are taken from their nests when they are still fledglings. Once they lose their fear of human hands and accept food, a "master nightingale" is borrowed and put near the fledglings. The master bird sings to the little birds every day. For about a month, the little birds listen to the master bird singing its lovely song. The little ones try to imitate the sounds of the master. This is the little birds' "talent education." The master bird is the teacher, the fledglings the students.

If the master bird is a good teacher, the little birds will grow up singing a clear, heart-stopping melody, the very best and truest example of the song of the nightingales. But if the little birds remain in their nest and are raised by wild nightingales, the song will not be nearly as pure or pleasing to the ear, because the little birds will imitate the inferior sounds of the wild nightingales. This is mother-tongue learning.

There is a lesson for us in the way the Japanese musician accepts students. Any child can enter Suzuki's Talent Education Institute without tests, because the Japanese violinist feels talent is cultivated, not inherited. The term "genius" as he uses it does not mean someone who was born with exceptional native abilities; it's a term of honor reserved for someone who is brought up and trained to have high ability.

According to the mother-tongue approach, the child

learns to play the violin (or the piano or cello) as easily as he learns to speak. Whether he wants to play or not is as irrelevant as asking the child if he wants to learn to talk; he learns easily, naturally, listening first to records, then imitating what he hears.

Talent or Environment?

But, you might be thinking, isn't a child who's very bright going to be a star anyway? Can't a child with exceptional native intelligence overcome an environment that doesn't encourage learning? Aren't the child's natural abilities going to develop anyway? Probably not, is the answer from child development research. Intelligence, like physical growth, needs nurturing. The brain, like muscles, has to be trained. John McEnroe would not have become a championship tennis player if he had not played tennis day after day after day, hours on end, set after set after set.

As early as 1863 a now-famous Russian physiologist by the name of Ivan M. Sechenov proposed that stimulation of the senses—the pathway to learning—is a process necessary to life. All of us need stimulation, and we need it most of all when we are small babies and our nervous systems are developing at a rapid rate. Interference with this process of natural stimulation, said Sechenov, leads to unhappiness and withdrawal from stimulating activity.

From the work of Sechenov and those who followed him, we know that newborn babies strive for sensory stimulation—of their eyes, ears, bodies and taste buds—and that as their striving increases, their behavioral response to greater stimulation also increases. In simple terms, the more a baby reaches out to grasp an object, the more able that baby is to grasp and hold the object.

But what if no one holds out a bright plastic ring for the

Early Learning: Why All the Fuss?

baby to try to grasp? What if no one smiles and encourages the baby trying to use his tiny fingers to hold the ring? The baby will not develop his grasp-holding abilities to the extent that he should. He will lose interest. He will lie listlessly in his crib. He will quickly develop a "Who cares?" attitude.

A child adapts to his environment, whatever that environment is. If the environment encourages learning and growth, the baby will learn and develop. If the environment teaches the child to walk on all fours and smear food in her hair, the child will do exactly that. A child who hears howls instead of human speech will howl, not talk—no matter how bright the child.

"To look at a school-age child with stunted or damaged abilities and say that this is inherited is a grave mistake," asserts Suzuki. "The destiny of children lies in the hands of their parents."

That destiny, which is shaped very early, is in good hands when parents realize how important their role as teacher really is, and how much they can do at home to make sure their children learn what they naturally want to learn. You do not need an expensive course on how to make your baby smarter, expensive toys that purport to teach mental gymnastics skills, and you don't need flashcards. You do not need to try to teach your baby how to read or print his name. In the final analysis, what does it matter if he learns to read at three, five, six, or seven, as long as when he does learn he develops excellent skills in understanding what he has read? Far more important than trying to teach your child *how* to read is to instill in him or her a love of and appreciation for books. Reading to a young child and showing him the pictures in simple books will help to prepare him for reading and make him *want* to learn to read, when the time comes (more on this in Chapter Six).

Remember, you are your child's first and most important teacher. Your child wants what *you* can give him, not what a flash card can give him. And what you can give him, it turns out, is plenty.

What Should My Child Be Doing— and When?

All parents wonder, and sometimes worry, if their children are developing normally. All children grow and develop at an individual pace; there are no rules that work for all children. For instance, your child may be a little behind other children his or her age when it comes to walking, but may be talking in an amazingly advanced way. The following charts will give you general guidelines on what children do at what age. But remember, they're only general guidelines. Your child will set the pace that works best for him or her. (Note that a premature baby will be a little later at doing some of these things than other babies. It doesn't mean the baby isn't as bright—just that he has to take a little longer to catch up.)

MOVING THE WHOLE BODY

Characteristics	*Most Babies First Do This Between*
Holds head off of bed for a few moments while lying on stomach	Birth and 4 wks
Holds head upright lying on stomach	5 wks and 3 mos
Holds head steady when held in sitting position	6 wks and 4 mos
Rolls over from front to back, or from back to front	2 mos and 5 mos
Sits without support when placed in a sitting position	5 mos and 8 mos

Early Learning: Why All the Fuss?

Gets into sitting position in crib or on floor without help	6 mos and 11 mos
Takes part of weight on own legs when held steady	3 mos and 8 mos
Stands holding on	5 mos and 10 mos
Stands for a moment alone	9 mos and 13 mos
Stands alone well	10 mos and 14 mos
Walks holding onto furniture	7½ mos and 13 mos
Walks alone across a room	11 mos and 15 mos

USING HANDS AND EYES

Characteristics	*Most Babies First Do This Between*
Follows an object with eyes for a short distance	Birth and 6 wks
Follows with eyes from one side all the way to the other side of head	2 mos and 4 mos
Brings hands together in front of body	6 wks and 3½ mos
Grasps a rattle placed in fingers	2½ mos and 4½ mos
Passes a toy from one hand to the other	5 mos and 7½ mos
Grasps a small object (like a raisin) off a flat surface	5 mos and 8 mos
Picks up a small object using thumb and finger	7 mos and 10 mos
Brings together two toys held in hands	7 mos and 12 mos
Scribbles with a pencil or crayon	12 mos and 24 mos

USING EARS AND VOICE

Characteristics	*Most Babies First Do This Between*
Pays attention to sounds	Birth and 6 wks
Makes vocal sounds other than crying	Birth and 6 wks
Laughs	6 wks and 3½ mos
Squeals	6 wks and 4½ mos
Turns toward your voice	4 mos and 8 mos
Says "Dada" or "Mama"	6 mos and 10 mos

Uses Dada or Mama to mean one specific
  person   10 mos and 14 mos
Imitates the speech sounds you make   6 mos and 11 mos

BEHAVING WITH PEOPLE

Characteristics	Most Babies First Do This Between
Looks at your face	Birth and 1 mo
Smiles when you smile or play with him or her	Birth and 2 mos
Smiles by self	6 wks and 5 mos
Pulls back when you pull a toy in his or her hand	4 mos and 10 mos
Tries to get a toy that is out of reach	5 mos and 9 mos
Feeds crackers to self	5 mos and 8 mos
Drinks from a cup by self	10 mos and 16 mos
Uses a spoon, spills little	13 mos and 24 mos
Plays peek-a-boo	6 mos and 10 mos
Plays pat-a-cake	7 mos and 13 mos
Plays with a ball on the floor	10 mos and 16 mos

NOTE: These charts are reprinted from *Infant Care*, a publication of the U.S. Department of Health and Human Services.

When Does Your Child Respond Most to Stimulation?

Like adults, babies have body rhythms and sleep/waking cycles that are unique to them. Keeping a record of sleep/waking cycles for your baby will help you be alert to the infant's own natural patterns of growth and development. If you know when your baby most appreciates playtime, you'll be less likely to interrupt necessary sleep and more likely to play when your infant is alert and really feels like some stimulation.

To help you pinpoint your baby's own natural sleeping/waking cycle, start keeping the accompanying chart. If

INFANT'S SLEEP/WAKING RECORD (By Month)

MY CHILD'S NAME: **AGE:** **MONTH:**

Day of Month:	Time Awake—A.M.	Time Awake—P.M.	Time(s) when child is most responsive to stimulating play
1			
2			
3			
4			
5			
6			
7			
8			

Continue chart on another piece of paper for the rest of the days of the month. Use of the chart for several months will help you tune in to your child's natural sleep/waking/play cycles.

you start when your baby is a newborn, you will find that your baby seems to sleep most of the time. As your infant grows older, you'll notice that the waking periods on the chart become longer and longer, and your baby stays alert longer. Timing your play to your infant's readiness for it will help you both enjoy it more.

2. Superbabies: Born to Learn

> We have made a kind of bargain with nature: our children will be difficult to raise, but their capacity for new learning will greatly enhance the chances of survival of the human species.
>
> —CARL SAGAN, *The Dragons of Eden*

Your child is a superbaby. He was born that way. He's a superbaby in the sense that he's a super learner. In his first few years of life he will learn more, faster, than he ever will again at any other time in his life. By the age of three, he'll have acquired about 80 percent of the basic knowledge he needs to cope in the world. Much of what follows will be a refinement of his existing knowledge base.

Your child is a natural learner in the sense that she's inquisitive, a toucher, a born explorer. She's curious about everything she sees, hears, eats, touches, eliminates. Your little explorer will learn whether you help the process along or not. But if you play an active role in your child's learning, your child will learn more readily.

Flash-card Whiz Kids

Playing an active role in your child's learning or being your child's first teacher doesn't mean you should try to rush your child into the kind of learning he'll get at school. That's not the point. You've probably read articles about parents who show their babies flash cards at the age of one to teach them how to read. "Flash cards at one! What are they thinking of?" the country's most famous pediatrician, Benjamin Spock, exclaimed recently at a national conference on single-parent families and schools held in Washington, D.C. "Children can only mature if they have stimulation," said Spock. "But is this [flash-card learning] a natural thing? If it's highly unnatural, I think children shouldn't be subjected to this."

The key to learning for a young child is the word natural. Flash-card learning is not natural. An active, wiggly young child does not naturally stand at attention to memorize words held up before her on a piece of paper. She isn't ready physically or emotionally for the kind of classroom learning approach she'll get in first grade.

Consider how babies and toddlers learn. Their major learning tasks center on exploration, first of their bodies and then of the interaction of their bodies with the outside world. What is a hand? This is a wonderful problem for a baby, occupying weeks of his alert time. How many fingers are there? How can they be moved in space? And then, What is a hand for? Can a hand touch something? Pick it up? Turn it over? There are endless experiments to be done. Now contrast this kind of natural exploratory learning to the flash-card approach. The cards are somehow forced on the child, rather than discovered. It's a little like watching television, rather than doing something for yourself.

There is a major difference between inactive and active learning. A very young child learns best by *doing*. In order to find out whether a metal spoon will make a noise when it's banged on something, your child bangs the spoon on a pan and hears the sound. In order to find out what will happen to a tall mound of sand when something heavy presses on it, your child will stand on top of the mound and feel it flatten beneath him. In order to find out what different objects or animals feel like, your child will touch them and find out about the roughness of sandpaper, the furriness of a kitten, or the smooth, slick surface of plastic. It is through these active experiences with things that your child begins to learn about ideas.

For example, your child learns the concept of "under" literally by placing one thing under another, such as one block under another or a toy under a book. What's remarkable about this exploratory process of learning by doing is that we all do things a little differently and thus form slightly different concepts about our world. No two people have exactly the same concept of "under" or "over."

In this way each child becomes a creative thinker. No one will ever see a sunset, draw a picture of you with crayons, explore the wild flowers of a meadow in the spring, or sing a song exactly like your child—ever.

Your preschool child doesn't think like an adult, nor should he. Lacking a wide experience with objects, ideas, and people, the child relates to the here and now, the concrete experience. A pencil is not appreciated by a baby because of what it can do—write words on paper—but because it is hard, can be picked up, put in the mouth and chewed. The abstract idea of what the pencil represents—writing—is not really part of the preschool child's world, although some young children will learn to write the letters of their names by repeating what an adult does. In that case, they're not really *writing;* they're imitating.

To understand the differences between how an adult thinks and how a child thinks, see the chart at the end of this chapter. The chart will help you understand that you cannot reason with a very young child in the same way that you would with an adult. It's meaningless to tell a preschooler that he will have to wait until 5:00 P.M. for dinner; he lacks the sense of time as an orderly, structured tool that divides the day into predictable segments. A child who is hungry wants to eat *now*, and has no concept of putting off his gratification until later in the day.

Trying to force adult learning patterns on a preschool child will only lead to frustration for both of you. It's far better (and more fun) to try to understand how your child sees the world and look at situations through the eyes of the child.

Learning or Precocity?

Trying to force your child's learning in unnatural ways, such as showing a child flash cards for hours, also raises the issue of precocity. A precocious child is a child who has learned early how to please adults by doing adult things. Early academic training can lead to precocity, and can teach your child to perform to please you, not him. "By giving too much academic training too early, you get the whole parent–child relationship lopsided" is the view of Spock. He points out that a child might quite logically begin to reason this way: "This is what my parents love me for—for being able to answer the flash cards." Implicit in that statement is "not for myself." And, in fact, having a precocious child is a way some parents reassure themselves they are "good parents." They can say, "Look how smart my child is. I must be doing something right."

When parents encourage precocity, they can actually hinder a child's development by ignoring things a child can't do well. "Kids avoid the things they can't do. Parents show them off on the things they do well," says University of Arizona educator Samuel A. Kirk, the man who is credited with coining the term "learning disabilities" in 1964. A child who is smart enough to avoid what he doesn't want to do by showing off on something that pleases adults (such as singing all the songs he knows for your guests) will fall into this pattern as a way of avoiding something else. If you avoid something, you can't learn about it.

In the bittersweet television film *The Summer of My German Soldier*, child actress Kristy McNichol plays a waifish preteen whose father resents her and favors her little sister. The little sister is a Shirley Temple clone with golden ringlets who is making a career of being precocious as a preschooler. She sings "five foot two, eyes of blue" and mugs for her adoring audience, whose most prominent viewer is her father. McNichol asks her, "Can't you see what they're turning you into?" What they are turning her into is a precocious exhibitionist. She is performing, not learning.

Flash-card learning also ignores the physical experience of learning by doing, your child's primary way of mastering tasks. Your child's mind is naturally guided by an irresistible biological drive to structure, organize, and complete experience—that is, to make sense of the world. This drive complements your child's natural sense of curiosity—the desire to explore with her body that sends her up on a chair to reach a vase of flowers and down on her knees to examine a caterpillar. She doesn't need to perform or show off to learn; applause for showing off is not what naturally motivates learning in a young child.

Much real learning—and your child's is no exception—involves the experience of "getting the hang of it" or "getting the feel of it," a trial-and-error process that leads to mastery. This process takes place at all levels of your child's nervous system, from purely physical sensation on up to sophisticated mental processes. Thus, learning to tie shoes or ride a bike or speak or write involves all levels of integration of the nervous system.

These tasks can't be formally taught on flash cards or in written directions but must be learned by doing, since much of the function and memory of mastering a task resides at the levels of the senses and muscles. The way your child structures and organizes his world will depend to a great extent on an active use of his senses. For example, our concepts of large/small, heavy/light, and far/near depend in large part on the memory in our bodies of how big something looked to us, what it felt like to move it, and how hard it was to reach it.

By encouraging your child to use her body and experience her world, you're encouraging the learning process. By helping her deal with the inevitable frustration when something doesn't go right—by taking a break, letting go of a problem—you're also helping her learn more effectively. When your child is caught in the problem of trying to reach for a toy under a chair and his hand won't reach, the child must be able to give it up, stop tugging, step back, and start again, walking around the chair and finding the shortest distance to reach and thus grasp the toy.

Finally, the rote flash-card approach to learning that ignores physical experience also tends to ignore the emotional side of your child's development. Early teaching that ignores your child's social and emotional growth might backfire later. It's like putting one part of your child's development—the fact-gathering part—on the fast track and ignoring all the other parts of your child that count, or putting them on hold. Your child is smart enough to want to learn in a variety of areas, at her own pace. Teaching that emphasizes only the mental or "cognitive" part of your child's growth process is incomplete and biased. It ignores feelings.

Head over Heart

Helping your child to experience and understand feelings is a major part of learning. If your child only learned words and facts and figures and abstract problem-solving techniques, he or she would be ill-equipped for living in the world.

A prime example of how and why it doesn't work to forget feelings for facts is British economic theorist John Stuart Mill. As a little boy, Mill was raised as a child prodigy. Bright, yes, but he had a nervous breakdown at the age of twenty. Born in 1806, the young Mill was reading Greek at three, Latin at eight, and logic at twelve. His father, James Mill, author of a weighty history of British India, was determined to provide his son with what he saw as "the highest order of intellectual education." While Mill senior toiled away on his voluminous history of India at a writing table, little John sat at the same table, asking his father what the Greek words he saw meant.

The education of John now seems to us humorless, loveless, and harsh. While the boy read Plato aloud, the father constantly criticized the way his little son read, often losing his temper. He told the boy how to read, but never showed him by example. The little boy, who was indeed very smart, dimly saw that his father was wedded to abstract ideas, not the here and now. But his suspicion wasn't enough to save him.

With a head full of Greek and Roman history, philosophy, mathematics, and logic, young Mill determined to reform the world. Like a mystic or a prophet, he dedicated himself to that abstract ideal: saving the world. At the age of twenty, in 1826, the young man woke up "as from a dream." He asked himself if he could be happy if his dream of saving the world were realized, and got back a "no." He then fell into a deep depression. "I seemed to have nothing left to live for." A good night's sleep didn't help. Young John's depression hung over him like a storm cloud before a heavy rain. His father, he felt, was the last person he could turn to for help.

John Stuart Mill saw that his analytical education under his father's hand had been conducted without any inkling that it could end in total hopelessness. John at twenty saw that cold-blooded analysis—using an intellectual chisel on the world—wears down feelings. Today we would say that John Stuart Mill was "emotionally deprived," even though he came from a "good" home. Consider how ignorantly at twenty he speaks of emotions such as love and tenderness: ". . . to know that a feeling would make me happy if I had it, did not give me the feeling." Precocious? Yes. Happy? No. Analytically advanced? Yes. Able to connect and empathize with others in a mentally healthy way? No.

What's the message for parents in the education of John Stuart Mill? An emphasis on mental achievement alone isn't enough. A child is not a computer. A child has feelings and wants. A child should be loved for himself, not for what someone stuffs into his head. A child is not a professional performer.

You probably don't have to be told your baby has feelings as well as an intellect, but it's worth noting that we're learning a great deal more about just how capable of feeling and expressing emotions an infant really is. The investigations into infant emotions parallel the growing research on the intellectual wonders of the infant's mind. Although we think of depression as an adult or young-adult problem (John Stuart Mill was a depressed young adult), infants can experience the same emotion. They experience this depressive response when they're separated from their mothers, for example.

In University of Massachusetts research studies of three-month-old infants whose mothers pretended to be depressed, the babies acted wary and then looked away when they saw their mothers' sad faces, becoming sad themselves in response to their mothers' expressions. A joyful little face smiling a greeting to an unresponsive, sad mother quickly became sad and withdrawn.

Babies clearly can also express anger from an early age, as judged by the looks on their faces and their general fussiness. And you don't need to be told your baby can express pleasure and joy.

Lessons from Neuroscience

Your child learns because she has a highly developed nervous system whose center is a sophisticated organ called the brain. The brain weighs about three pounds when it's fully grown. It is composed of nerve cells and nerve fibers, and on the inside it looks like a convoluted relief map, a mass of intricate little humps, hills, and valleys. The human species now dominates the world because our brains are larger (as a proportion of total body size) than they are in any other species. Inside the human brain, there is the potential for more connections among individual nerve cells than all the atoms in the universe—and those connections, biologically, are what we know as thinking.

Recently, researchers who specialize in neuroscience have made major advances in their understanding of how people think. They've learned, for instance, that neurotransmitters—messenger "thought juices" that allow one cell in the brain to communicate with another—are much more complex and sophisticated than they had imagined. Scientists used to think that one brain cell, or neuron, secreted only one neurotransmitter, but recent studies by National Institute of Mental Health researchers Thomas O'Donohue and his wife, Gail E. Handelmann, have shown that a brain cell is capable of secreting several different neurotransmitters from the two dozen or so that have been discovered. Why would one brain cell secrete more than one "thought juice"? No one really knows yet, but what this discovery means is that thinking, which at its fundamental level involves communication among brain cells, has many more potential biological pathways than scientists had supposed. Understanding thinking at this biochemical level may make it possible to explain why some stroke victims who have lost massive parts of their brains make remarkable recoveries. In these people, new thought pathways seem to be taking over for the old.

Even a very simple organism "thinks" in the sense of reacting to its environment. Columbia University researcher Eric Kandel has found, for instance, that a humble little marine snail, the aplysia, thinks to the extent of becoming anxious about a potential threat in the world outside it and taking steps to protect itself from that threat. He found that a physical shock to the head of this simple but savvy snail actually stimulates cells in the snail's nervous system to secrete a substance called serotonin. That might not seem so remarkable until you realize that serotonin is one of the chemical neurotransmitters—thought juices—found in *human* brains and important in *human* thought.

We're clearly in the midst of a revolution in our understanding about how the brain works, a revolution which may someday affect your child.

How the Brain Works

When your child thinks, nerve impulses—little electrical discharges—travel from brain cell to brain cell. The electrical impulse moves down the nerve fiber (axon) of the cell until it comes to the end, where it finds many branches like the branches of a tree, forming thousands of possible connections with nearby nerve cells. When the nerve impulse comes to the end of the fiber, the nerve ending releases a neurotransmitter, whose messenger action bridges the gap (called a synapse) between nerve cells. The nerve impulse can be transmitted across this gap only through the release of chemical thought juices, which then migrate to adjacent cells and set up nerve impulses there. The major part of the brain, the part where higher thinking takes place, is called the cerebral cortex.

Your child's brain is also, of course, a center for more than thinking. The brain serves as a kind of major information center for sensations coming in from outside, such as sights and smells; it controls movement, by signaling muscles what to do; and it controls the automatic functions of our bodies, the ones we rarely have to think about—breathing, the heartbeat, blood pressure, digestion of food, the regulation of body temperature, and more.

The brain is made up of two halves. In general, the right half controls vision, movement, and sensation for the left side of the body, while the left side controls vision, movement, and sensation for the right side of the body. But the brain isn't just two symmetrical mirror images. In general the left side of the brain is considered to be the one more involved with logic and rational thought, while the right side of the brain is believed to be more a center for creative and artistic efforts.

To understand how complex the internal communications network of the brain really is, consider that one nerve cell may receive information from thousands of other nerve cells and at the same time has the capacity to transmit information to many thousands of additional nerve cells. The brain is far more sophisiticated than any computer yet built. The number of circuit shift-registers (places where an electrical current changes direction) in a complex computer may approach the tens of millions. But in the human brain, there are hundreds of billions. The mature human brain is far more jam-packed with information, and with potential ways of making sense of that information, than any computer.

You may have been reading lately that female brains are different biologically from male brains. The brain's two halves are called hemispheres. Currently researchers believe that the left hemisphere of the brain is more responsible for auditory and language skills, while the right hemisphere is more responsible for spatial and numerical skills. Scientists believe that while the two hemispheres of female brains may be rather equal in function, boys may have a dominant right hemisphere, the part of the brain where skills in solving mathematical and spatial problems are developed. Anatomically, the part of the brain that connects these two hemispheres—called the corpus callosum—is larger and wider in females than in males. What researchers now think may be happening is that the two halves of women's brains communicate more readily than the two hemispheres of a male brain, perhaps because the enlarged and widened "bridge" of the corpus callosum allows signals to travel back and forth between the two hemispheres more efficiently.

Boys traditionally have always done better than girls in mathematics and spatial relations, although of course there are some girls who are mathematical whizzes. And girls traditionally have always done better than boys in verbal communication, although of course some of the best actors and writers have been men.

Anyone who has ever watched little girls and little boys play in a group has noted that in general the boys tend to play more aggressively and physically, while little girls tend to sit with a parent or with another girl and play quietly. Unquestionably, these differences in play styles are the result of male and female hormones, not just cultural differences in how we raise our children. The physical differences between male and female brains, which are probably also the result of the different actions of male and female hormones, may help to explain why boys are generally better in math and girls are better at verbal communication.

An important study published in *The New England Journal of Medicine* adds persuasive evidence to the notion that sex hormones affect how boys and girls think. Physicians Daniel B. Hier and William F. Crowley, Jr., compared nineteen men who were born eunuchs—their bodies didn't have enough male sex hormones—with nineteen normal men. They found that the eunuchs had dramatically lower spatial ability than the normal men, as measured by standard spatial ability tests. The researchers aren't exactly sure why male sex hormones have such an important effect on the brain, but they note that the male sex hormone testosterone plays an important role in how the central nervous system is organized.

If you have a little girl, maybe all this sounds sexist to you, and maybe you're concerned that this biological difference will somehow affect her intelligence. But the truth is that biological differences in male and female brains may account for certain tendencies or skills, but *not* for intelligence per se. For example, female babies tend to be more sensitive to sounds from birth than male babies, which isn't surprising since females tend to be more verbal as they grow older.

The study of how brain biology affects brain function is still very new, and it doesn't explain everything. If your little girl shows a preference for numbers and not letters as she grows older, by all means encourage her; she may grow up to be a mathematician or an engineer. But if she prefers words and communication through talking, she may be expressing a tendency that is rooted in biology, and that's fine, too.

The Biology of Stimulation

There are a lot of good psychological reasons for stimulating your child to learn. Your child will be more ready for school. Your child will be better able to play in a friendly, social way with his or her playmates. Your child will develop inner resources so he can entertain himself with games, puzzles, and learning toys. But laboratory research studies also indicate there's a sound biological reason for stimulating your child to learn: in laboratory experiments, stimulated brains grow bigger and heavier.

In studies with rats at the University of California at Berkeley, two populations of laboratory rats were kept: one group in a dull, uninteresting environment, and another in a stimulating environment. The group that received special mental stimulation actually showed a measurable increase in the size and thickness of the thinking center of the brain, the cerebral cortex. While it's always risky to make a jump from laboratory rats to people, we have to take on faith that at least some of what's been demonstrated about rat brains also applies to children's brains.

What's the value of a biologically more developed brain? It's likely that a "weightier" brain has more of the apparatus necessary for thinking: more connections among nerve cells, indicating more potential thought linkages.

The Brain's Vulnerability

Joseph Altman, a professor of biological sciences at Purdue University, believes there is an external germinal layer of the brain with neuroblasts (precursors of nerve cells) that persists in a young child up to the age of two. It is the transformation of these important neuroblasts into brain cells that biologically governs your child's potential as a thinker. These neuroblasts, which move out of the germinal layer and migrate to different parts of the brain, along with the nerve cells themselves, are highly sensitive to any kind of traumatic effect, such as a blow to the head or malnutrition. Injured or food-starved neuroblasts might not develop into full-fledged nerve cells.

The human brain needs to do most of its growing while a child is an infant and toddler, since the brain will approach its adult size, weight, and mature quota of cells by the age of two. As National Institute of Child Health and Human Development researcher Merrill S. Read has pointed out, a child's major brain-growth spurt occurs extremely early in life: from the fourth month of fetal development to six months of age. Since this is the time when brain cells multiply rapidly and grow, it's not hard to see why it's so important for your child's brain to be well nourished during this period. The brain growth spurt continues at a slightly slower pace until about eighteen to twenty-four months of age.

The brain growth spurt of a baby can be viewed in two stages with two major functions. The major purpose of the first stage, when the baby is still a fetus, is to increase the number of nerve cells in the brain. As we saw, a nerve cell, called a neuron, is the major working unit in the brain. When brain cells "talk to" each other, thinking takes place. During the second major growth spurt, which extends from the sixth month of pregnancy through about six months of age, support cells of the nervous system called glia multiply. Also during this stage, those treelike branches (called dendrites) from already established nerve cells grow to form the connections (synapses) over which nerve impulses will be conducted.

These two brain-growth stages overlap, so that many nerve cells are still multiplying after birth. And the sophisticated processes of forming dendrites and synapses, which allow complex communication among brain cells, are probably more important to human mental functioning than the mere *number* of these nerve cells. In the case of the brain, the number of connections seems to be more important than the number of connectors.

Throughout all this important growth, the brain needs nutritious food to do its work. Studies in laboratory animals show that severe malnutrition can produce brain deficits which can't be overcome later, even if the animal is eventually put on a good diet. Rats that are severely deprived of nutrients during the first stage of the brain growth spurt, when they're still in the womb, don't develop as many nerve cells as other rats. An extremely restricted diet during the second stage of the growth spurt, while animals are nursing, actually produces a rat brain that's smaller in diameter as well as reduced in cell number. Since the regions of the brain grow at different rates during the extended growth spurt, malnutrition at any one period could affect a specific part of the brain most severely, thereby affecting the functions of that part of the brain.

The Malleable Organ

Stimulating your child's brain to grow to its full potential while your child is still young is especially important when you consider that mature nerve cells don't divide to make new nerve cells. In other words, you want all the neuroblasts your child was born with to develop into nerve cells in order to achieve full mental potential. The adult brain seems to have the capacity to regenerate connections between nerve cells, which may at least partially explain why stroke victims with brain injury can learn to talk or walk again. But lost nerve cells themselves essentially remain lost; they *never* grow back.

It used to be thought that nerve cells were formed, made connections to each other, and developed into an adult brain in an orderly way that was preprogrammed by heredity. But now neuroscientists know that theory about neat and orderly preprogrammed progression won't hold up. The discovery of neurotransmitters and their functions is revolutionizing brain science. For instance, neuroscientists are learning that neurotransmitters can stimulate and direct the growth of nerve cell processes to specific target cells.

It's impossible to say now what effect the conscious, planned stimulation of a child's brain will have on the intricate biology of nerve cells and neurotransmitters. We do know, however, that experience can modify the communication among nerve cells in specific ways that control the physical properties of the nerve membrane and the secretion of those neurotransmitters, or thought juices. If normal experience can modify brain communication, it seems likely that learning experiences at a young age can also modify brain biology.

Just as we've learned that the body's immune system,

our internal disease-fighting mechanism, doesn't function totally independently but is governed by the brain (more on this in Chapter Eight), so we may discover that learning is governed by specific neurotransmitters or specific nerve cells. And if early learning proves to have a direct, measurable effect on brain biology and brain growth in children as well as in laboratory animals, then infant stimulation will have a clear scientific rationale.

Many scientists think it already does.

HOW TO UNDERSTAND YOUR PRESCHOOL CHILD'S THINKING

Your child's thought can be described as prerational, similar to what Freud termed "primary process thinking," thinking based on unconscious thought processes. Piaget later used the term "preoperational" to describe children's thinking; that term suggests the illogical, idiosyncratic nature of children's thinking. The following table illustrates the differences between adult and child thinking; there is, of course, some overlap between the two.

Child	Adult
free association (flight of ideas): "Where's teddy bear, I'm hungry, these are my blocks . . ."	*linear, step-by-step approach*: "I'll preheat the oven, take down the pie pan, sift the flour . . ."
concrete, often visual: "Mommy is putting water and something white into a big red bowl."	*abstract, often verbal*: "I am following a pie recipe as it is written down in steps."
timeless: "It has been forever since I ate."	*sequential*: "I served lunch at twelve noon, and now it's already four o'clock and time to start dinner."
wish fulfillment (thought and action the same): "I see the pie I want pie I eat pie."	*delay of gratification (wish subordinate to thought processes)*: "Dinner is served in courses; I will serve the pie later with coffee."
egocentric (unclear boundary between self and others): "If I'm hungry, I should be fed, right NOW!"	*socialized (awareness of relationships between self and others)*: "I am cooking a meal for my family as well as for myself. We will eat it together in an hour."

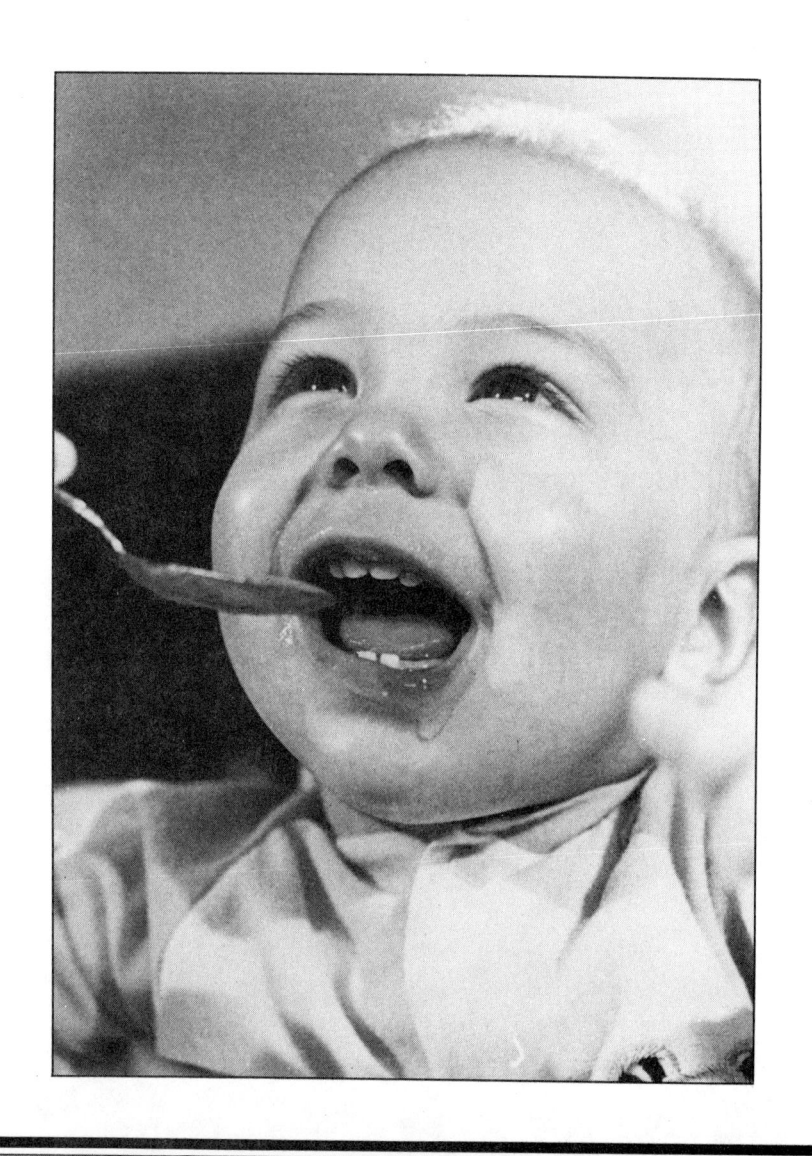

3. The Senses: Doors to Learning

If I had only . . .
forgotten future greatness
and looked at the green things and the buildings
and reached out to those around me
and smelled the air
and ignored the forms and the self-styled obligations
and heard the rain on the roof . . .
—HUGH PRATHER, *Notes to Myself*

Equipped with a rapidly developing brain that's making millions of important internal thought connections, your child is a naturally voracious learner. But where does he get all the information to make the thought connections? Through his five senses. Eyes and ears are your child's main doors to learning. They will also be your child's major tools in speaking, reading, and manipulating numbers. If she has normal vision and hearing, learning for her will be a rich feast of green leaves, yellow sand, blue waves that break in froth, birdcalls, telephone conversations, fire bells, and nursery rhymes.

Your baby can see, hear, and make sounds at birth. The middle and inner ear begin developing in the third week of pregnancy and most of the structure of the ear is complete by midpregnancy, even though the cartilage will continue to harden throughout pregnancy and after birth. Many researchers now believe that a human infant can actually hear during his last three months in the womb, even though he's surrounded by amniotic fluid.

A baby's eyes develop during the first three months of

pregnancy. The retina, the innermost part of the eyeball, continues to develop throughout pregnancy and after birth. Most specialists believe a baby's vision can be accurately measured by three months of age, even though specific aspects of vision continue to develop through the first years of life.

A baby's world assumes meaning and structure first passively, though his or her senses. Your face and voice become linked to the breast or bottle, with being held and rocked. These events, called "sensorimotor" experiences, evoke certain pleasant feelings of "being cared for." So the concept of mother and father develop and grow throughout childhood, from those first sensory experiences. These early physical and emotional experiences of being parented are so varied that no two people have exactly the same concept of mothering. The way it felt to be held in your mother's arms—gently or stiffly, clumsily or firmly—contributes enormously to your concept of mother. Those early experiences will also contribute to the child's concept of father.

Your baby's first major challenges come from trying to see, hear, and touch things in a new and unfamiliar world. As she grabs for and then shakes a rattle, plays with her toes, and tries to crawl, the senses become the child's means of mastering her environment. That's why saying "Don't touch" to a baby is really the equivalent of saying "Don't learn." You wouldn't tell a child "Don't hear," "Don't smell," or "Don't see." The child is a scientist-explorer using the tools he has—his senses—and through a process of trial and error he finds out what he can do by doing. By doing, he masters the unfamiliar world in which he has found himself.

Numerical Harmony

Recent research has taught us that even small babies have a mechanism, a kind of inborn knowledge base, that allows them to draw very basic conclusions about numbers. They can't count, but they seem to have an innate, rhythmical sense of what number is.

A study of infants between the ages of six and eight months showed that the babies could actually make a connection between the number of sounds they were hearing (such as drumbeats) and the number of objects they were looking at—an amazingly sophisticated feat for a child under one year of age.

Prentice Starkey, Elizabeth S. Spelke, and Rochel Gelman, psychologists working at the University of Pennsylvania, showed pictures of grouped household objects (such as coin purses, water glasses, gloves, pillows, and eggbeaters) to sixteen babies between six and eight months old. Then, while showing the babies the grouped objects, the researchers banged on a drum, using different combinations of drumbeats. They found that the babies looked longer at pictures that contained the same number of objects as the number of drumbeats they were hearing.

For example, when the babies saw a display of two objects, such as a wooden bowl and a lemon, they looked at the bowl and lemon longer if they heard the accompanying sound of two drumbeats as opposed to three. In fact, the majority of the babies tested preferred looking at the same number of objects as the number of sounds they were hearing, showing that they liked the correlation of visual objects and sounds. In effect, the babies seemed to appreciate the harmony of matching visual objects to sounds in a kind of numerical pattern.

Amazing? Yes, especially when you consider that a seven-month-old won't officially learn to count until much later. The implications of babies' numerical awareness and sophistication are staggering, even though we don't yet know whether they can really *understand* the difference between two and three in the same way older children do. It's possible, the researchers concluded, that what babies understand is not two versus three, but one object versus many objects. In other words, they can make a distinction between one apple and a group of apples—whether two, three, ten, or twenty.

The point is that babies are aware of numbers, in a kind of sensory way, even if they can't yet count, just as they're aware of words even if they can't yet talk. And the more scientists find out about the degree of this awareness, the more impressed they are with the sophistication of a baby's brain.

Color Them Smart

It used to be assumed that babies see only in black and white, mainly because they seem to react most strongly to and prefer high-contrast images in black and white, such as checkerboard squares. But now we're fairly certain that children as young as two or three months can distinguish some colors, if not the entire subtle color spectrum adults see. In studies with four-month-old babies, New York University psychologist Marc H. Bornstein has found that babies prefer the colors pure red and pure blue. How could he tell? They looked longer at these colors than they did at blended colors, such as blue-green (turquoise).

A recent study from McMaster University in Hamilton, Ontario, showed that even newborns apparently have a

The Senses: Doors to Learning

rudimentary sense of color. Researchers Russell J. Adams and Daphne Maurer set up an experiment with thirty newborns in which they tested whether the babies could recognize color. They relied on the knowledge that babies prefer high contrast, and will look longer at a checkerboard pattern with contrasting colors than at a square of all one shade with no contrast or at a pattern that has little contrast. The researchers made checkerboard patterns of green-gray checks and checkerboard patterns of gray-gray checks, carefully matching the luminance (intensity) of the gray checks in the second type of pattern to the luminance of the green checks in the first pattern. If newborns could not distinguish color, then they should not have been able to tell the difference between the two types of patterns: green-gray and gray-gray. However, in every case newborns looked longer at the checkerboard patterns contrasting green with gray checks. Since babies prefer contrast, and since—if the green could be seen—green-gray presents a higher contrast than gray-gray, the researchers concluded that the newborns could actually detect the color green.

If, as research is showing us, young babies do prefer primary colors, then the pink and blue pastels of most nursery equipment will have to be rethought. These pale colors seem to appeal most to adults, for whom they evoke a sense of fragility, tenderness, and the vulnerability of the newborn. But if the baby himself prefers pure red and pure blue, then a pale-pink baby blanket will have to give way to, say, a quilt with squares in strong primary colors. And since babies like high contrast, timid wallpaper patterns and pale flowered prints should give way to brighter patterns babies will find more stimulating.

Learning through Sight

A healthy, bright child is a voracious sampler of new sights. To imagine what it feels like, think back to when you saw a seashore, a zebra, a mountain range, or a ferris wheel for the first time. To a young child, the world of sights is a constant delight of newness: everything is a wondrous discovery and a visual treat. Three important visual skills are needed so that your child can process, or make sense of, what he is seeing: focusing, conjugate gaze, and tracking.

Focusing is simply the ability of the eyes to see an object clearly at various distances; conjugate gaze is the ability of both eyes to fixate on the same object at the same time; and tracking is the ability to follow an object as it moves (or later, in school, to direct the eyes across a written page or down a column of numbers).

A newborn can see accurately at a distance of about eight inches. The newborn can focus his eyes—but only when he's alert, not when he's sleepy. To encourage a baby to focus, hold an object about seven to eight inches away from the baby when he's alert, not when his eyelids are drooping from drowsiness. By the time a baby is a month old, she can track an object, in the sense of following it with her eyes. To encourage this important tracking skill, hold an object off to the side of the baby's head (we sense movement better off to the side) and gradually bring it in front of the baby. She will move her head and track the moving object with her eyes. By three months, a bright, healthy baby is a champion tracker, and by seven or eight months vision is well developed in most infants.

How good your child's eyesight is—whether she has 20/20 vision or not—isn't really directly related to how well she

The Senses: Doors to Learning

will learn. The term 20/20 vision describes the ability of a person to see a letter of a certain size at a distance of twenty feet. Many children with learning disabilities have 20/20 vision, while many children who are fast learners don't have 20/20 vision. They either wear glasses or sit up front, in an instinctive compensation for eyesight that's less than perfect. What does count in learning is not whether your child has 20/20 vision, but how well she can focus, coordinate her eyes, and track an object.

To get a sense of how important vision is to a young child with a lot to learn about himself and his world, stand on one foot and close your eyes. Tough, isn't it? But if you open your eyes, it becomes a lot easier. Vision helps your child orient himself to everything around him.

Processing new information through the eyes is a form of highly sophisticated mental gymnastics for your young child. He has to run through no less than the following six major processing steps:

1) receive a stimulus, such as a color pattern made by a brilliantly colored rotating pinwheel;

2) become oriented and move the head and eyes toward the stimulus;

3) scan the object providing the stimulus, in this case a pinwheel;

4) identify the major visual cues of the object (shape, size, color, motion);

5) integrate these visual cues into his brain;

6) classify the object (in this case, he'll decide that the pinwheel is a toy, not, say, something to eat like a doughnut).

As you can see, visual processing is an extremely complex task for a baby or toddler, especially when you consider how much of what he's seeing is completely new to him. While you know immediately how to classify a pinwheel, because you've seen it before, a baby looking at a pinwheel for the first time must go through a complex process of elimination and categorization to get some idea of what this strange new object really is. Since it's been estimated that between 75 and 90 percent of all classroom learning gets to the child's brain through her eyes, you can see how important it is for a child to use her eyes as learning tools beginning when she's a newborn.

Your child's eyes are her first and most important means of understanding objects in her world. When you show your child a simple picture book with familiar objects in it, you're helping her orient herself to her world through the use of images. These images are symbols that capture reality in the fast-moving world of a child. Being able to relate an image to its real counterpart (sometimes called visual perception) is an important skill a child must develop before she gets to school.

Visual perception allows the child to relate experiences she has had in her short life to the pictures on a page. Visual perception is an important tool for helping her decide what things are, what they mean, and how she should act according to her interpretation of what they mean. The images your child sees have the power to convey meaning to her. For example, a child who has taken a plane trip and then sees a picture of an airplane in a picture book will be stimulated simply by the image of the plane to think about travel and distance: an airplane allows me to visit Grandma, who lives far away. The reason that it's so important to show your child simple picture books from the time he's a toddler is that they help him develop visual perception.

In addition to the skills the eyes themselves must develop, your child must begin to use his hands together with his eyes so he can develop eye/hand coordination. When

The Senses: Doors to Learning

a child reaches for something, for instance, his eyes are sending him signals and his hands are carrying out instructions from his brain. The important teamwork of eye/hand coordination is essential if a child is going to learn to read and write.

When you give your child a learning toy that asks her to fit an object into a particular space—for instance, a wooden board puzzle—you're encouraging her to develop eye/hand coordination. When you give her crayons and let her draw, you're also encouraging eye/hand coordination. And you're encouraging the growth of tiny hand muscles that will be needed when the child gets to school. Almost any active toy or task that demands concentration will involve a high degree of eye/hand coordination. A child who goes to school without developing eye/hand coordination will be at a distinct disadvantage compared to children who have worked on this important skill.

Ears on the World

Next to your child's eyes, her ears are her most important sensory learning tools. Hearing is essential to a young child's development because it's through hearing that she acquires speech, and it's through speech that she communicates with those around her. While bright children who are deaf from birth can learn to talk, it's extremely difficult for a child to learn a language she's never heard others speaking. The American Speech–Language–Hearing Association has broken down the learning of language into a series of seven major steps that begin at birth. Consider how important your child's ears are as she goes through the process of learning to talk.

1. *Newborn:* Listens to speech; startles or cries at loud noises; awakens at loud sounds. Coos and gurgles.

2. *Three months:* Tries to turn toward a speaker; smiles when spoken to; stops playing and seems to listen to sounds or speech; seems to recognize mother's voice. Babbles; cries differently for different needs, such as hunger or a wet diaper; repeats the same sounds over and over.

3. *Six months:* Responds to "No" and to his or her name; notices new sounds and looks around for their source; turns head toward the side where the sound is coming from. Babbling sounds more like the parents' speech, only not clear; the child makes lots of different kinds of sounds.

4. *Nine months to one year:* Turns or looks up when you call; searches and looks around when hearing new sounds; listens to people talking. Enjoys imitating sounds; uses jargon (baby babbling that sounds like real speech); uses his or her voice to get attention.

5. *One and one-half to two years:* Follows two requests, as in "Please go get the ball and put it on the table"; has ten to fifteen words in his or her vocabulary by the age of two; sometimes repeats requests, as in "Get ball"; asks one- to two-word questions, such as "More?" "Where kitty?" "Go bye-bye?"; shows the ability to put two words together, as in "More cookie."

6. *Two and one-half to four years:* Clearly understands differences in meaning, such as the difference between "go" and "stop"; points to pictures in a book when he hears them named, such as "dog" or "apple"; understands and interprets sounds around him, such as a dog barking, a telephone ringing, a television program, a doorbell's ring; understands others' conversations; seems to hear the radio or television at about the same level as the other family members. Has a vocabulary of several hundred words or more (some children have one-thousand-word vocabularies by this age); uses two- to three-word sentences; asks lots of questions that begin with "why" or "what"; has largely

The Senses: Doors to Learning

stopped talking in jargon and repeating sounds; likes to name objects; is able to say most sounds, except perhaps *r*, *s*, *th*, and *l*; sometimes repeats words in a sentence.

7. *Five years:* Hears and understands most speech in the home; hears and answers when first called; hears quiet speech; appears to hear well, according to others who know him or her (grandparents, teacher, babysitter). Says all sounds correctly except perhaps *s* and *th;* uses the same sentence structure as the rest of the family; talks in a clear voice, as clear as other children the same age.

It's clear from looking at these seven stages that in a normal, bright baby learning to talk is largely a function of hearing and listening. In order to learn to talk eventually, a baby must hear the speech of adult human beings, just as a small bird must listen to the song the adult bird sings. The baby has to become accustomed to the sounds of human voices speaking to each other, to pitch, and to the rhythm of words. Since children will not grow up to talk baby talk, it makes little sense to talk baby talk to a child, who will then come to imitate that—not adult speech. What does make sense when talking for the benefit of a baby is to slow speech down, repeating sounds so the child can become accustomed to them.

In general, your child will first learn nouns—the concrete names for people, objects, and animals. Adults can help this natural noun-learning process by pointing and saying what things are: "See the dog." "Look at the flower."

It's not surprising that your child learns language by mastering nouns first when you consider that verbs express relationships between things and people, a far more complicated concept than simply naming things and people. The verb "to run," for example, doesn't mean much to your child until he learns what runs and where it runs to: a girl runs home, a boy runs around the bases, a dog runs into the lake to fetch a stick, a man runs a marathon through the streets of Boston.

Your child will generally start using language that sounds like the spoken word between the ages of one and three, and he will develop his skills at his own pace. By the time he's reached the age of two, you'll probably be able to understand about half of what your toddler says. By the age of three, his vocabulary will probably be somewhere between 500 and 1,000 words and he'll be able to understand the meaning of perhaps 2,000 words, even if he doesn't use them all.

If your child seems to be slow in developing speech, it may simply mean he's spending time on other things that interest him more. Some children are very slow to develop speech, perhaps because they are more interested in carefully observing their natural surroundings than in talking about what they see. But a child who says no words at all by the age of two may not just be taking his own time in language development; he may have a hearing problem, and your pediatrician might want to recommend that you consult a hearing specialist for tests.

Ear infections are extremely common in toddlers and young children, and recurrent ear infections can cause some hearing loss if they're not treated. Major hearing losses are fairly easy to pick up now with the proper diagnostic tests; minor hearing losses that could interfere with language learning are less easy to pinpoint. You may have heard your pediatrician use the term "otitis media," which simply means middle ear infection. Next to colds, middle ear infections are the most common childhood ailment. These troublesome infections can cause your child's ears to become stopped up with fluid.

Doctors have several approaches in treating otitis media—decongestant and antihistamine drugs, antibiotics, and drainage tubes implanted surgically for stubborn cases. Otitis media can and should be diagnosed and treated as early as possible. If fluid remains in a child's ear for more than three months, the child will probably have some hearing loss, and that loss could interfere with language development. Today doctors can successfully test hearing as early as infancy, using special equipment.

Why Do We Learn to Talk?

Why does a bright child with normal hearing learn language at all? Is there something innate in your child that makes her want to speak with other human beings?

Research on fossilized remains of early manlike creatures gives us a clue to why human children learn to communicate by speaking rather than, say, by sign language. The remains suggest that the human larynx—the physical tool your child uses to talk—gradually developed into its present size and shape through millions of years of evolution. Without the larynx, there would have been no tool for a highly developed language in human beings.

The advantages gained from precise communication must have exerted enormous pressure on the evolutionary process. Through natural selection, mutations which produced a more and more sophisticated vocal apparatus were passed on to succeeding generations. In simple terms, the larynx and vocal cords became larger and better, allowing humans to talk better. At the current state of evolution, we can say that talking is about as natural to your child as breathing.

Language is a social act as well as an intellectual means of making something known or finding something out.

Talking helps your child share his thoughts and needs with others, and learn who he is and where he fits in with the world.

A human baby who coos and gurgles needs to hear speech before his own vocal tract is really developed enough to produce intelligible words. In that sense, babies aren't too different from other species. For example, the white-crowned sparrow needs to hear his own unique birdsong from mature sparrows during his first year of life, or he won't ever learn the song of the white-crowned sparrow properly. Like a song sparrow, a baby needs to hear your speech to develop his own.

Research shows that babies can *understand* the sounds of speech on a basic level long before they can *produce* such sounds themselves. An infant can discriminate between very similar sounds even if she can't say them herself. For instance, a baby as young as one month can distinguish between the consonants *p* and *b*, even if she can't say them, notes psychologist Norman A. Krasnegor, a specialist on human learning and behavior with the National Institute of Child Health and Human Development. A baby makes many of these phonetic discriminations with his brain a full year before he can produce them in his own speech.

A newborn can identify his or her mother's voice from other voices, indicating the baby can hear and recognize the mother's voice while still in the womb, Krasnegor has noted. (Reports that babies can learn symphonies while still fetuses, although intriguing, haven't been proven; learning a symphony is a giant step from recognizing the sound of your mother's voice.)

Not talking to a young baby is a mistake some highly intelligent, well-educated parents make quite understandably, Burton White has found in his observations in the home. Most of us think of talking in terms of having a conversation: you say something, then the other person says something, then you say something back, and so on. Your baby obviously can't participate in a conversation, but that doesn't mean she doesn't want to hear, or can't respond to, your voice. You may initially feel a little silly carrying on a one-way conversation with a tiny bundle that looks at you but can't join in with witty, punchy remarks.

As your baby grows older and sleeps less and less, you'll be rewarded for your one-way conversations with the child's increasing alertness: head movements, eye contact, and the beautiful, wide, toothless "social smile" of babyhood.

Why Talk to Your Child?

If you doubt whether all that conversational effort during your child's infancy and toddlerhood is really worth it, consider the results of an extremely important study on young children and sounds done by two British psychologists at Oxford University. Lynette Bradley and Peter E. Bryant studied 368 preschoolers who could not yet read. They trained and measured the children's ability to categorize sounds and their sensitivity to rhyme (through words like cat and hat) and alliteration (repetition of the same sound in nearby words, such as woolly and wonderful) before they could read.

The researchers followed these children for four years once they got to school to see how well they did in reading and spelling. What they found was that the children who had acquired a strong sense of sounds before they got to school did far better on reading and spelling in school than children who came to school lacking what the researchers termed "phonological awareness." Where do babies and toddlers get this sense of sounds? From parents who talk to them.

It's unusual for respected scientific researchers, who are naturally cautious, to be overly enthusiastic about their conclusions when they write up their research results. Usually they qualify their conclusions. Then they often add that the subject "needs further study." But Bradley and Bryant were so convinced of the strength of their findings they couldn't help but be positive. They concluded in a report in the prestigious scientific journal *Nature* that "the awareness of rhyme and alliteration which children acquire before they go to school, possibly as a result of their experiences at home, has a powerful influence on their eventual success in learning to read and to spell." The two British researchers believe that their study is the first to show that a child's preschool awareness of the sounds that make words is a direct cause of success in reading once that child gets to school.

Bradley and Bryant weren't the only ones who were enthusiastic about their study. In an analysis of their study published in the same issue of *Nature,* psychology professor Max Coltheart of the University of London was equally enthusiastic about their conclusions. Coltheart said their study "provides the first clear evidence of the mental procedures important in the early stages of learning to read."

For hundreds of years specialists have debated whether a child learns to read by a sort of abstract word-specific reasoning process that depends on what a child has already learned about a particular word, or by a phonetic process that depends on relating particular letters or groups of letters to spoken sounds (for example, the *at* in cat, hat, bat, and mat). People who favor the phonetic approach to

The Senses: Doors to Learning

learning to read try to link the written word directly to the spoken word, by helping and encouraging the child to say the written word aloud to see what it sounds like.

While it's probably a mistake to assume that all children learn to read the same way, the phonetic way, the British study does make a convincing case for the phonetic route to reading success. It also makes a convincing case for beginning that route very early—when a child is still a baby. If the route to reading is through hearing sounds, then imagine what an advantage a child who has already been exposed to a great variety of sounds in spoken language will have once he gets to school. And, in contrast, imagine what a great disadvantage the child who has heard very little spoken language will face.

In their study, Bradley and Bryant divided the children into two groups before they learned to read: one group that received no special training in sounds (but did have training in the abstract categorization of words), and a second group that did have word-sound phonetic training. The children in the second group, which received the word-sound training, learned to read far more easily than children in the abstract-reasoning training group.

This study is important not only because it shows children with a better phonetic awareness of words learn to read more easily, but also because it shows that parents and others who work with children before school should make an effort to interest children in sounds themselves. It's worth noting the kinds of techniques the British researchers used to relate sounds to objects.

For instance, they showed children colored pictures of familiar objects or animals and taught them that different words for these objects often shared a common beginning letter (*h* in both hen and hat); a common middle letter (*e* as in hen and pet); and a common ending letter (*n* as in hen and man). The researchers also showed the children plastic letter shapes for *h, e,* and *n,* so they would begin to become aware of what these letters looked like as members of the alphabet.

The British researchers weren't trying to teach the children "how to read."

They were preparing the children to learn to read in a natural way so that the task would be easier once they got to school. Reading is thus seen as the natural culmination of the child's growing awareness of sounds and the spoken word. This is a lot different from showing a child of one or two a flash card with "hen" on it and expecting the child to learn to read the word hen in a book.

Language awareness, like all the experiences a child has with his senses, should be fun. A child learns easily that words can be fun when he hears amusing words, points out Susannah M. McCuaig, a South Carolina educator and reading specialist. "Bumblebee," which almost sounds like the buzzing of a bee, is an example, she notes.

Although we've talked mostly about sight and hearing in this chapter, don't forget touch and taste when thinking of your child's senses as doors to learning. Offering your child a little taste of a new food is an important new learning experience for her, even if she doesn't like what she tastes. Finding out what's rough, what's furry, or what's smooth is also an important learning experience, especially because it can generate the "why" questions important to gaining new knowledge. Why is a caterpillar woolly? Why is a fish scaly and cold to the touch? Why does a dog have fur? Why do people have smooth skin on their tummies and hair on their heads?

Computer Learning: Using the Hands to Read

Children usually learn to read before they learn to write, but it doesn't have to be that way, contends educator John Henry Martin. In fact, feels Martin, it works better the other way around, when children have typewriters and computers to help them.

We've seen in this chapter that children learn through their hands, touching and feeling their way to an understanding of their world. Martin, who is convinced that children's hands are the gateway to their brains, extended the concept of hands-on learning to reading. In 1975 the former teacher and principal retired to Stuart, Florida, with an idea simmering at the back of his mind he wanted to try out. He thought children could learn to read faster if they could do it through their fingers—actually create the letters for the words they were trying to learn to recognize.

Martin had a research basis for his theory: a 1932 book called *An Experimental Study of the Educational Influences of the Typewriter in the Elementary School Classroom,* coauthored by a man he much admired, Benjamin Wood. Wood had found that children were fascinated by machines, loved to touch the keys, and learned readily when they could use typewriters.

In September 1977 Martin tried out his theory with the loan of some International Business Machines (IBM) Selectric typewriters at a research laboratory in the Martin County, Florida, public school system. Some 126 children in five first-grade classes began what has come to be called the writing-to-read program in classes lasting thirty minutes each day. Instead of laboriously making letters on paper with pencil, they learned to peck out words on the typewriter, words they could see on paper.

The writing-to-read program took off from there. Children learned to type out stories and to read what they were writing. IBM executives were so impressed that in November 1980 the company placed an ad in *The Wall Street Journal* that said, "Should Johnny Learn to Type Before He Learns to Read?" The ad went on to say that Martin had "achieved dramatic results with this experimental program. After the first seven months all his students can read and write, and over half can read more than a year ahead of their grade level. . . ."

Martin decided to expand the writing-to-read program to include microcomputers, reasoning that they could add a great deal to the learning process because a computer can be programmed to respond to the user. In 1981, Martin copyrighted a teaching method using a computer with a viewing screen and a typewriter keyboard. The writing-to-read system was expanded beyond the boundaries of Florida to more than one hundred schools in seven states. IBM lent the equipment and published the program's materials based on directions supplied by Martin.

The personal computer used by a child in the program has a voice attachment and comes with diskettes that allow the child to type words and get a picture on the screen. For example, there's a bed with a green blanket and red pillow and the word "bed" beside it, a white rabbit with a cotton tail, and a yellow fish. The child listens to tape-recorded instructions, uses his fingers to type, then sees the picture of the object or animal along with the word for it—so he or she is using the sense of hearing, the sense of touch and sight in combination to learn. Students also say the words, and teachers help the children learn to pronounce the words they are learning.

The Senses: Doors to Learning

Martin believes the physical involvement in learning—the active participation of the senses—is what helps children learn to read. It's quite different from sitting with a book and trying to look at letters and memorize their combinations. The writing-to-read program is currently being evaluated by other educators.

For further information about the writing-to-read system, contact IBM Corporation, Department 8P1, P.O. Box 1328, Boca Raton, Florida 33432. A summary article on the program by Pamela Hawkins appeared in the December 1982 issue of *IPD News*, which is published by IBM's Information Products Division, White Plains, New York 10601 (Volume 1, Number 3 issue).

How to Encourage Whole-body Learning

Your young child learns about her environment through use of the whole body—exploration by touch, movement, doing something physical. Here are a few tips for encouraging whole-body learning at home:

For a baby:
1. Push on your baby's feet, encouraging a kick response (the same reflexes will later be used for walking).
2. Hold your finger out for your baby to grasp; most babies have a surprisingly strong grasp reflex even when they're very tiny.
3. For a baby just learning to crawl, put down a large clean sheet or blanket and put a number of objects on the sheet (blocks, toys with wheels, soft animals) for your baby to explore as she's crawling on the sheet.
4. Put your baby in a molded baby seat (you can

use most infant car seats for this) so that she can be with you and see what's going on in the room; a baby left in her crib all the time misses out on what is going on around her.

For a toddler:
1. Show your child how to look at the world upside down by bending over and looking through your legs; your child will probably imitate you, since children love to do as you do. Most children love the sensation of looking at the world upside down.
2. Crawl under a table with your child (he will probably follow in fascination) to give him the experience of being under something. Raise your hand and gently bang the top of the table over your head. It's through experiences like these that your child learns the concepts of under and over.
3. Watch your child develop her hand/eye coordination by stacking blocks on top of each other. Now try alternating in placing the block—you put one on, then she puts one on. In addition to teaching your child about balance and size (blocks in graduated sizes build a higher tower), alternately placing the blocks is fun, and begins to teach your child cooperation and sharing.
4. Buy a sturdy rocking horse so that your child will get a feeling for the motion of rocking, a whole-body sensation. This will prepare your child for sitting on a tricycle when he's older and pedaling with his feet.

4. Stimulation: How Much, How Often, What Kind?

> It is a superior environment that has the greatest effect in creating superior abilities.
>
> —SHINICHI SUZUKI, *Nurtured by Love*

Because we now know so much more about a baby's capacity for learning, child development specialists are becoming increasingly convinced of the importance of deliberate stimulation, beginning at birth and continuing through toddlerhood and the preschool years. But it's important to remember that your baby is an individual with her own personality and temperament. That personality and temperament, along with the child's natural curiosity and playfulness, will help to determine how much stimulation you give, what kind, and how often.

Harvard University pediatrician T. Berry Brazelton has identified three types of infants, all perfectly normal: quiet, superactive, and somewhere in between. Just as adults do, babies have their own styles, their own body clocks and pacing, their own likes and dislikes. And they also have their own ways of developing. One baby will walk at eleven months, but may say few words before two. Another may walk late, but will be babbling away at sixteen months. One toddler will be content to sit on the floor working complicated puzzles longer than you thought he could sit still, while yet another child will move around the room at top speed like a human tornado. All of these children are simply learning at their own pace, according to their own temperaments. To try to fit them into a learning mold (which doesn't exist anyway) would be unproductive and insulting to the child's individuality.

Before launching a program of planned stimulation for your new baby, try to tune in to the child's personality and unique signals—remembering that a new baby will naturally spend most of her time sleeping. A sleepy new baby isn't necessarily a baby with a quiet personality; she's just doing what comes most naturally to newborns. Pick a time to stimulate her when she's awake, alert, dry, and fed.

When your baby is alert and comfortable (not sick or fussy), notice how much she moves around. Does your three-month-old wiggle all over the crib or stay pretty much in one place? When you change a diaper or slip a nightshirt over your baby's head, does he move around and stretch or stay still? Both the wigglers and the quieter babies are perfectly normal. One is not necessarily brighter than another because he is more active. However, you might want to stimulate a wiggler a little differently from a quiet dreamer.

If you have a super-active wiggler who kicks and squirms and seems to be a dynamic little bundle of energy, the main problem is helping him learn how to slow down and concentrate. You can do this by moving and talking a little more slowly yourself, and by setting an example of paying attention. If, on the other hand, you have a very quiet baby, you may want to set a more active pace, and encourage him in his busy-ness and his activities by letting him know that what he does is terrific. In this supportive way, you'll be encouraging your quiet little dreamer to become more of an active self-starter.

Stimulation: Strictly Individual

Whether you have a super-active dynamo or a quieter infant, it's important to gauge the type and length of time you spend in infant stimulation to the abilities of your growing baby, keeping in mind the wide variation in how babies develop. To get a general idea of what your baby can do turn again to the charts at the end of Chapter One. They'll give you an overall idea of the age range during which your baby can sit without support, will grasp a rattle placed in his hand, and will try to get a toy that is out of reach.

The times when you have physical contact with your baby—feeding, diaper changing, and bathing—are perfect times for infant stimulation. Look into your baby's eyes when you pick him up and handle him so he can come to know your face; the top half of a human face—especially a parent's—is a baby's favorite sight. Infant stimulation advocates such as Susan Ludington recommend taping a black-and-white photograph of yourself on the side of your baby's crib so your baby can see you when you're not there.

Babies like contrast in what they see: black-and-white checkerboards and bull's-eyes are examples of patterns that appeal to babies because they have strong contrast. In addition to gazing into your baby's eyes, you can stimulate his sense of touch during feeding or diapering: gently push against his hands; hold him in a sitting position, supporting his head with your hand before he can do it for himself. Hug, kiss, and stroke your baby, and don't worry about spoiling him with all the physical affection. Babies need a great deal of touching, which is your way of expressing caring.

Between birth and six weeks, hold an object such as a

rattle about eight inches from your baby's eyes and move it slowly so he will follow it with his eyes. Remember that following an object with the eyes (tracking) will encourage him to learn to focus his gaze, a skill he will need for almost every kind of learning. Somewhere between two months and four months, if he's learned to track early, your baby will learn to follow an object with his eyes by moving them from one side of the head all the way to the other side, a sophisticated skill for a baby. These are skills that will be extremely important when your baby starts learning to read in school.

Just as he prefers your face to all other sights, so your infant will prefer the sound of your voice to all other sounds. Talk to your baby as often as possible, speaking in short, full sentences and pronouncing words correctly.

Stimulation: More Is Better

As your child's very first and most important teacher, you will be giving your baby a lot of planned stimulation, and helping her organize a new and bewildering environment. Imagine what it would feel like if you had spent all of your life in a dark, secure, comfortable place surrounded by warm, soothing water, getting all the nourishment you needed without effort. Then imagine that you were abruptly seized from your comforting environment and thrust into a world of bright lights, loud, jangling noises, and cold drafts of air, a strange world in which you had to make sure your own basic survival needs—for food, dry clothing, and rest— were met. How would you cope? Once upon a time you did, and that formidable task is exactly what your baby is called on to do now.

Although the barrage of stimuli that confronts your baby seems bewildering, babies are uniquely equipped to re-

Stimulation: How Much, How Often, What Kind?

spond to stimulation selectively and to let you know when too much is too much (see the checklist at the end of this chapter). In general, too much stimulation is far better than not enough. We know what happens to babies who aren't given enough human stimulation from observing infants raised in orphanages who aren't given enough individual attention.

At about the age of two months, these babies, like all babies, reach out, grasp an adult finger, touch objects, ask for human contact, and smile engagingly at adults. But when they find that despite all their best and most social efforts they don't get attention and prolonged closeness with an adult in return, they become listless, apathetic, and withdrawn. They become helpless, with no sense that what they do matters—since what they do doesn't get a response.

Stanley I. Greenspan, a psychiatrist with the Mental Health Study Center of the National Institute of Mental Health and an expert on how babies adapt to their new and bewildering surroundings, has pointed out that caring adults are indispensable in the baby's process of finding out what this strange world is all about. Just as a baby who's hungry or wet will cry for someone to come and feed or change her, so a bright, normal baby wants an adult to celebrate joyfully with her as she follows an object with her eyes for a short distance, learns to roll over or hold her head up off the crib mattress for a few minutes while lying on her stomach. These are early explorations of the bewildering new world, and caring parents will not only encourage them but help them along.

A parent who values stimulation starting in infancy is first of all a highly responsive parent. Sarale Cohen, an assistant professor of pediatrics at the University of California School of Medicine (Los Angeles), has come up with a way of defining responsive caregiving that says a lot about why the babies of responsive parents learn about their world faster. While it's difficult to dissect responsiveness, she's broken it down in the following way.

The responsive caregiver of a one-month-old infant is one who:

1) spends a high percentage of the time the baby's awake touching or holding the baby, talking to the baby and looking into the baby's eyes while the baby gazes back;

2) spends a lot of time face to face with the baby;

3) talks to the baby a great deal of the time while facing her;

4) holds the baby often in the upright position (on a shoulder, for example);

5) generally responds to a baby's fussiness or crying within forty-five seconds.

The responsive caregiver of an eight-month-old is one who responds to his or her baby in similar ways, except that the parent responds to the baby's babbling sounds by talking back (preconversation) and, instead of holding the baby in an upright position, lets the baby crawl on the floor.

The responsive caregiver of a two-year-old, Cohen has found, is a person who:

1) not only touches and talks to the child but presents a toy and plays with him;

2) sets up reciprocal situations with the baby, such as two-way "conversations" or rolling a ball back and forth between them;

3) encourages a child to look at books, listen to records, play with sand, water, and blocks and take part in pretend play with situations that aren't real (such as pretending to be in a castle).

Being responsive isn't really very difficult considering how engaging babies are. It's harder if there are other children at home, of course, because you have so many

Stimulation: How Much, How Often, What Kind?

distractions. When you change, bathe, or feed your baby, look closely into his eyes as much as possible; he will reward you by meeting your gaze. Remember, his favorite object is your face, and he needs to look and look and look. When you turn your face away while you care for your baby, you deprive him of what he most wants to see.

Your baby will also respond to your voice, since the human voice is his favorite sound. When he "talks" to you, talk back, speaking distinctly and slowly. Play music for him, and watch him turn his head toward the sound of the music box. Shake a rattle gently near your baby's ear and watch him react.

Getting Physical

A young child's body needs stimulation as much as his brain. When your baby kicks her legs, encourage her by smiling and clapping your hands. Press gently on the soles of her feet when her knees are bent to encourage her to thrust her legs out in a kick.

Esther Thelen and Donna M. Fisher of the psychology department at the University of Missouri in Columbia believe that infant kicking exercises a combination of muscles which will later be needed for upright walking. When they studied the kicking of babies between five days and six months old, Thelen and Fisher found that kicking could be divided into four distinct phases. First the baby moves her leg toward her body, simultaneously flexing the ankle, knee, and hip. Then there is a pause, which represents the second phase of the kick. The third phase is the extension phase, as the baby thrusts and straightens out her leg. Finally, there is another pause, an interval between the first kick and the next. Babies' kick patterns were quite individual, the researchers found; different babies had varying times of flexion, for example. Intervals between kicks could vary from less than a second to several minutes in length, although individual kicks by all the babies studied tended to cluster together in spurts of movement separated by nonkicking intervals. Thelen and Fisher theorize that the baby's nervous system may actually convert knowledge of muscle coordination learned in spontaneous kicking motions into the knowledge that will be required to walk. In that sense, spontaneous kicking is transformed into the voluntary, willed actions of walking.

Other groups of muscles that will need to function as a unit are being exercised as your baby rocks, waves, bounces, bangs, and sways. Muscle knowledge comes with muscle use, and your baby needs to be active. Encourage efforts at motion by smiling, patting a striving little body, and rocking the baby in your arms.

Most of all, your baby responds to your touch. Stroke your baby from head to toe several times a day, and let him feel your hands soaping his body when you bathe him. Shop for a baby carrier that lets your baby rest against your body so you can take her shopping with you and even do housework without losing touch.

When Michael and Ann Moore of Evergreen, Colorado, were in Africa serving with the Peace Corps, they noticed that African women used their shawls to carry their infants with them everywhere they went. Ann, a nurse, felt this African tradition of love and physical closeness held an important message for Western parents. Using her experience as a pediatric nurse and mother, Ann Moore designed a soft baby carrier called Snugli, a little fabric sack which holds the baby on the parent's chest or back while leaving the arms free. The Snugli carrier has padded shoulder straps, and a reinforced head support to cradle the baby's delicate head and neck. Ann likes to say that Snugli was

Stimulation: How Much, How Often, What Kind?

designed "to hold your baby as close as a hug." The importance of a good baby carrier is that it lets you "hug" your baby while also letting you get dinner, make a bed, or simply sit and read while your baby sleeps—a heartbeat away.

A number of parents have taken their babies to infant swim classes for children under one year of age sponsored by groups such as the YMCA. Babies and young children love water, and most (but not all) will welcome a chance to paddle—with a caring adult supporting the middle with a strong hand. Infant swim classes can be marvelous for your baby's development—if they're well supervised.

"It is critically important that parents understand the safety factors involved as they involve their infants and preschoolers in an aquatic program," cautions Louise Priest, executive director of the Council for National Cooperation in Aquatics, Inc., a public service organization. "There are excellent programs in the U.S. . . . However, there are also some programs which do not stress safety factors, and which give parents both unrealistic expectations regarding the value of the program to their preschooler and safety factors involved."

Before enrolling your infant or preschool child in an infant swim class, ask to visit. Is the supervision good enough to suit you? Are pool-shy children encouraged to go in the water or forced? Do the children look happy? If the vibrations you're getting aren't good ones, look for another class or stick with your bathtub at home.

When Enough Is Enough

How do you know when too much stimulation time with your baby is too much? Simple: your baby will let you know. When a normal infant has had enough play and enough learning time, she will turn her head or whole body away and her back may arch rigidly. She may start to cry or push the toy away, just as she pushes a bottle away when she's no longer hungry. You've probably seen exactly this resonse in your own baby. In general, infants will respond to adult stimulation with smiles and an intent look that comes from riveted attention. If you're not getting this response, simply stop the stimulation and let your baby rest.

Morton Silverman, director of the preschool program at the Emma Pendleton Bradley Hospital in East Providence, Rhode Island, which is affiliated with Brown University, notes that a healthy, rested baby of about three months will begin to look forward to stimulation time with his parent with a look of alertness and movement of the body when the parent approaches. A baby anticipating the joys of playtime with you may reach toward you and smile when you come in the room. If you're not getting this response, your baby may be tired, ill, cranky, or just not in the mood. Just as you're not always in the mood to go to a party, so your baby doesn't always want to be "on" in his crib.

If you become tuned in to the signals he's sending you—a smile of anticipation or a head turned away—you'll know when to go full steam ahead and when to stop. Never force a baby who doesn't want to play right now, thank you. That's sure to bring crying and fussiness. Respect your baby's moods and desires and your baby will reward you with responses that make you certain your child is a genius.

Toddlers: Both Trying and Terrific

As your child moves into her first and then second year of life and starts to walk and make simple imitative sounds that will lead to talking, your role as teacher/stimulator

Stimulation: How Much, How Often, What Kind?

becomes more challenging. A bright, healthy toddler is capable of a lot of learning and a lot of mischief, as anyone who has cleaned lipstick and powder off the floor knows.

If your child is a toddler, you've no doubt noticed how, with great glee, he will delight in peek-a-boo games and tease you into chasing him. When you do, with mock seriousness, your child will duck under a chair or into a closet to hide. Later, as you're sitting there loudly asking, "Where's Peter?" and scratching your head, Peter will delightedly sneak up on you and pounce, landing in your arms.

The healthy toddler is capable of far less engaging behavior. Greenspan has observed in his studies that an angry toddler can be mischievous in a plotting, deliberate way. A toddler may leave his toys scattered all over, arrange for himself or his parents to trip over them, and then pretend to be upset, notes Greenspan. Is the toddler who does this Machiavellian? No—just smart. He doesn't do such things to be mean to himself or others, only to get a reaction.

It is at the toddler stage that your child will begin to play with toys in a way that indicates she knows exactly what they're used for and that she can, in an almost uncanny way, mimic adults using the toy's real counterparts. A toddler who has watched his mother or father sweeping may sweep with a toy broom and say "Uh, oh," when something lands on the floor (just like Mother or Father) and rush to sweep it up like one of Snow White's helpful seven dwarfs.

If your toddler has a toy telephone, you may have had the slightly unnerving experience of walking in the room to see the child on the floor happily dialing and carrying on preconversations in his own language. Listen closely and you'll probably notice that in tempo and inflection these one-way conversations bear a startling resemblance to adult conversations, even though the words aren't all there.

At this point, stimulation time gets a little more demanding and a little more complex. Because your child can do more and express herself more forcefully (often with a "No, no, no"), you'll also want to do more. At this stage of your child's development, you can not only enter into a game with her, but you can skillfully guide the game by letting your youngster shift it to suit her moods. Then you can reorganize the game if things get too chaotic and unsettling.

To get an idea of how adapting stimulation time to suit your youngster can work, consider this example from Stanley Greenspan: You and your child may begin your time together by looking at pictures of animals in a simple cloth book. Your toddler may suddenly shift his interest away from the horse in the picture (which he has just pointed to) and entice you into a chasing game.

You shift right along with him, putting down the book and pretending seriously to search for Johnny, who has disappeared. "Where's Johnny?" you ask, as Johnny, bursting with glee, hides in a closet. But Johnny may then get disorganized, running around and flailing his arms, overly exicted by the chase. So to help him gain a sense of organization and stability, you might soothingly settle him down by catching him in your arms, giving the squirming little body a gentle hug, and returning to the picture book and looking at the pages with him. You're back at the point where you started the stimulation time together: a quiet session, sharing the wonders of a book.

Because your child has more receptivity to language than language skills or actual words at this stage, you'll want to describe for her in simple terms the animals she's looking at, pointing to the picture in the book and then looking at her face. Help your youngster turn the pages for herself,

Stimulation: How Much, How Often, What Kind?

thereby encouraging the use of the hands to develop fine motor coordination. You can also encourage your child to point out the different parts of the picture after you describe them, thereby helping your child develop speaking skills and a large vocabulary.

Moving Toward Independence

All normal parents experience some conflicts about the extent of stimulation they provide their children—and the effects of such stimulation on the child as he grows older. The conflicts stem from a paradox: part of the parent wants a baby to remain a cuddly, dependent baby, while the other part realizes it's essential to help the baby grow into an independent, capable human being. Infant and child stimulation takes the child away from the parent in the sense that it helps the child become a competent person in his own right. In his work with the parents of toddlers, Greenspan has noted the following common parental fears triggered by the toddler's startling new capabilities:

1. The fear of being rejected or abandoned.
2. Concerns that the child is taking over and "becoming the boss."
3. Concerns about a child's personality based on misreadings about his increasing abilities.

Since the ultimate goal of stimulation is to foster competence and independence, what your child learns will inevitably take her away from you more and more. As she becomes absorbed in her own growing capacity to do things (and later, in schoolwork), her explorations will take her farther and farther from the parent's lap.

Some mothers enjoy having a baby who is almost totally dependent on them for every need, as a baby pretty much is during the first year of life. A mother who prefers a cuddly lap-sitter (who doesn't enjoy cuddling a baby?) may resent it or fear rejection when that lap-sitter starts moving around the house pulling pots and pans out of the kitchen cupboard and makeup off the dresser. The answer to such fears? A healthy respect for the child's growing abilitites and achievements, and pride in the realization that you're doing everything you can to make them possible.

Parents who perceive a normal, developing toddler's sense of initiative as a "strong will" and her independence as a willful "trying to be boss" may place too tight a rein on the child. It's like trying to restrain a high-spirited horse and keep the horse "in his place." The answer? Again, a very real sense of pride that you're helping to nurture a bright, active, independent child who can take initiative and who will later be able to take care of herself.

A parent may also misread a child's increasing capabilities as a sign that the child is developing an abnormal personality. For example, one fairly unassertive father, concerned he was nurturing an aggressive, hyperactive son, told Greenspan, "You've got to tame him early." While horses may need "taming" or "breaking," your child obviously doesn't. This father misread his bright child's initiative and sense of discovery as evidence of a lack of control over his son.

The result? "Not surprisingly, this very competent, industrious youngster became negativistic, belligerent, and disorganized in his aggression," comments Greenspan. "He alternated between disorganized aggressive play and clinging behavior." The solution? Instead of trying to block the bright child's attempts at initiative and assertiveness, give him acceptable channels, such as roughhousing games on tumbling mats, finger painting, and climbing on a jungle gym while you stand by, ready to help.

Of course you have to set limits for your increasingly independent and competent toddler; for example, while you might allow finger painting with washable paints on a kitchen floor, you wouldn't permit it on the living room rug. But it helps to remember that it's normal for healthy toddlers to be curious, exploratory little busybodies with ten fingers in ten different pies.

Signs of Readiness for Infant Stimulation

1. Your baby looks at you wide-eyed and eagerly when you enter the room.
2. Your baby focuses his gaze intently on your face as you come up to his crib.
3. Your baby reaches out his arms or kicks his feet in anticipation of playtime.
4. Your baby reaches eagerly for a toy if you hold one out and focuses her eyes on the toy.
5. Your baby smiles or gurgles happily.

Signs Your Baby Has Had Enough Stimulation

1. Your baby arches his back.
2. Your baby turns her head away from you.
3. When you hold a toy out to him, your baby pushes the toy away with his hand.
4. Your baby turns her whole body away from the person stimulating her.
5. Your baby cries fussily, indicating she has had enough and wants time to rest quietly or sleep.

5. More Than Child's Play

And does it not seem hard to you,
When all the sky is clear and blue,
And I should like so much to play,
To have to go to bed by day?

—Robert Louis Stevenson,
A Child's Garden of Verses

From the time your child is very tiny, she or he will delight in free, unrestricted play. She will play with her toes, with a bottle, with a kitchen spoon, with a pacifier, with a mobile—and with you. Play is as instinctive and natural to an intelligent, healthy baby as eating when he's hungry or sleeping when he's tired. All young animals—puppies, kittens, bear cubs—play instinctively. Does your child need to play? Is child's play an important part of learning? The answer to both these questions is yes, based on what we know from recent research on the phenomenon of play.

Play is the spontaneous activity of a developing child, through which he discovers himself and the world. It is the trial and error exploration of the universe, repeated by every human being. It's not a frivolous waste of time; it's the way your child makes sense of everything around him. It is through play that your child develops his entire view of the world.

Play Builds Competence

Why should you encourage your child to play? What is the value to your child of creating imaginary worlds with blocks, dollhouses, toy soldiers—or with nothing at all but a pile of sand? The joyful, spontaneous, and voluntary act of playing builds concentration the child will need later in school. When your child is involved in play, he is concentrating—just as you would concentrate if you had to write a complicated letter or read a weighty book.

This process of mental concentration in children's play is what University of Chicago human-development professor Mihaly Csikszentmihalyi calls "flow." In the case of truly enjoyable play, "going with the flow" can be such an intense experience that your child may not really hear or pay attention to anything around him. Such concentration-building through play can be valuable later, when powers of concentration will be required for schoolwork, and still later for the different requirements of a demanding job.

Play is not a means to an end but is undertaken for its own sake, without thought of reward, so play also fosters an internal sense of motivation. She plays because she wants to, not because someone tells her to. Being motivated and being able to fulfill that motivation, by playing at what she wishes exactly as she pleases, can help to develop the kind of motivation that a child will need later to stick with more complicated or frustrating tasks.

Play helps a child learn to complete tasks. Completion is inherent in the healthy, bright mind. Completion gives a sense of order to what a child does. Putting the last block on top of the pile, the last piece in the puzzle, gives the child a sense of completion and accomplishment.

A child whose playtime is always interrupted, who can never finish her sand castles or pile her blocks as high as she wants to, may find her natural sense of motivation and order quashed. Free play is important to a child because it gives her a chance to develop a sense of accomplishment herself—apart from adult approval. That helps her begin to develop a sense of competence, initiative, and self-esteem apart from what others tell her about herself. Eric Berne, the physician who developed a popular type of psychotherapy called transactional analysis, has described what happens to a child who is continually influenced by and directed by his parents as a series of compromises. The result is what he has termed "the adapted child." Children whose natural desires and impulses are continually repressed or channeled in different directions from what the children intended may in the process of adapting lose their capacity to feel for themselves, to be intrigued by the world around them, or even to give and receive affection, point out transactional analysis consultants Muriel James and Dorothy Jongeward.

The child who, on the other hand, plays naturally, exercises her own desires, and responds to her own impulses is not being an adapted child, in Berne's terminology, but a natural child. She is learning to do what pleases her, not someone else. She is not learning to feel pleasure and a sense of accomplishment simply because a parent says, for example, "You built a beautiful sand castle."

"Some children learn to comply in order to get along," write James and Jongeward in their book, *Born to Win*. But a child who is allowed to play naturally and freely will not have to comply with anything during playtime except the terms he sets for himself. The transactional analysis practitioners believe we take the child ego states—both the adapted child and the natural child—into adulthood with us. To the extent that we are able to retain the creative, happy, unrestrained part of the natural child we knew in free play, we can continue to feel a sense of sheer delight in accomplishment—apart from what a boss, spouse, or co-worker says about what we have done.

Playing for Joy

In a way, it seems almost self-defeating to try to define play scientifically, a little like trying to analyze the dust on Tinker Bell's wings. Undaunted, some researchers have stated that play, like reading, is a direct method of learning, a means of gaining factual knowledge. Others believe what counts is the spontaneity and randomness of play; in other words, when children play they initiate explorations of their world that help them find out more about that world and themselves incidentally or accidentally in the process. Some researchers believe in a kind of "play-competence spiral": as the child learns from his play, he plays in a more sophisticated way, which leads to more learning, which leads to more sophisticated play. In effect, when a bright child plays, he or she can't help but learn.

Play can be defined to the extent that it has certain unique characteristics that differentiate it from schoolwork or a chore. Play is done for its own sake rather than as a means to an end—getting a good grade, for instance. Play is spontaneous and voluntary, something your child chooses to do without being forced into it. A child who suddenly decides he's going to be a bear and go hide in a "cave" is celebrating the joyful spontaneity of play. No one has ordered him to go be a bear and hide.

Play is, above all, fun; the child who is truly playing may laugh out loud and clap his hands for the sheer joy of it. It has been said that play is the work of the child, but that's misleading because it implies a lack of enjoyment. True play is always fun. Play that lacks enjoyment is not play at all. Play is only work in the sense that it is part of the important process of what the child needs to do to learn. If

More Than Child's Play

your child is truly playing, he will be having fun, and it will show.

Daniel N. Stern, a psychiatrist at the New York Hospital–Cornell Medical Center, has described a wonderful kind of "play duet" that takes place between a mother and her baby when both are clearly having fun. What happens is that both start vocalizing in unison, the mother using words and the baby using the sounds in his pre-speech vocabulary.

During the play, especially when it's stimulating and highly arousing to the baby, they're both "talking" to each other at the same time to let the other one know how great the experience is that they're sharing. It's a little like chanting in unison at a football game—"Push 'em back, push 'em back, harder!"—when the audience gets into a unified state of excitement and shares the experience of the game, notes Stern. In the case of mother and baby, they're often gazing deeply into each other's eyes while they're making these sounds in unison.

Stern, who calls this kind of vocal sharing during play "coactional vocalizing," believes vocalizing in unison is an expression of "joy or shared delight in being with someone." This kind of shared delight can draw parent and child closer together. In this way, play becomes a means of sharing the sheer joy of being alive.

Child psychologists have been studying play for years as a vehicle to determine what's going on in a child's brain, using the device of play as a kind of psychological microscope. Urie Bronfenbrenner, a professor of human development and family studies at Cornell University, argues that we ought to look at play as an outside world created by the child and believed by him to be quite real. As he puts it, "We have developed elaborate and workable schemes for analyzing the human mind but not for describing the environments that the mind creates." A child is capable of creating the most exquisitely detailed, intricate environments in play. To him, they are extremely important, and they are extremely real.

During play, a child starts to learn the necessary but complicated process of distinguishing fantasy from reality. Children who learn from playing about what is real and what is not, as opposed to learning by watching television (more on that in the next chapter), quickly learn limits and boundaries naturally.

A child who pretends to be a monster, takes a block, and hits another child on the head quickly finds out that it hurts the other child because he cries or hits back. He gets a reaction, and the reaction helps him know how to behave. The child learns from the other child that it's O.K. to be a monster, but you can't really hit your victim because the child playing the victim doesn't like it and may hit you back. You have to *pretend* to hit the victim.

In play, children can take different roles. They learn what it feels like to be a victim as well as the monster. The child, whose world is completely egocentric, not emphathetic, can then begin to think of it this way: would I like to be hit on the head?

Parents and Play

Parents who value play as an important part of a child's life recognize that most bright, healthy children will naturally choose activities, games, action toys, or puzzles that are a little too difficult for them. Why? The most internally rewarding play is the play that provides your child with a challenge, and he knows it. A bright child will seek the toys that have complicated puzzle pieces to fit into elusive parts, or toys that require him to press a lever or button to get an effect. A bright preschooler will choose toys, games, and activities he feels he can do—but that he finds just a little bit too hard.

In a 1976 Harvard University study of "competent" children, those who were considered to be the best problem solvers came from homes that valued play. The homes of these children had exciting toys and the kind of learning tools you might find in a preschool: crayons, blank paper, blunt-tipped scissors. Blunt scissors might be considered dangerous for two-year-olds, but the competent toddlers were allowed to experiment with slightly dangerous toys—even if they made a mess.

The competent children were also allowed to participate in household jobs: dusting, raking leaves, sorting laundry, washing dishes. For these children, their play was all the more enticing because it was just like what Mother and Dad were doing. They did not feel excluded from their parents' adult lives; they were playing at the household chores their parents were doing for real. Even though a two-year-old can't really "wash" dishes and may make a puddle on the floor, mothers in the "competent homes" in this study allowed their toddlers to wallow in soapsuds up to their elbows.

You can help in this play-competence process by trying to match toys and play experiences to your child's abilities—at the upper end of those abilities. Toys are the fizz and the fun of growing up, what Burton L. White calls the "epsom salts" of early childhood education (see the list of toys you already own at the end of this chapter).

Choosing your child's toys is an important part of being a concerned parent. A toy for a one-year-old might bore a four-year-old, while a toy for a four-year-old might simply frustrate a one-year-old. Many toys now come with an age range printed on the box.

Unfortunately, some toy selection is bound to be hit-or-miss. This may be because the toy company misjudged the age range or put too wide an age range on a particular toy. A toy company that puts on the box "birth to three years" is obviously simply trying to get the most dollars from the largest group of parent-buyers. An infant and a three-year-old have different tastes in toys just as they have different physical and verbal abilities. Your child may also be ahead of other children in his or her age range when it comes to toy awareness.

And remember that toys that are aesthetically pleasing to adults may look "funny" to children. Many beautifully designed European toys (more on them later) come in lovely unfinished wood with the grain showing. But some children will feel the toys look "unfinished" and will want to paint them, to the horror of adults. A young child obviously doesn't have the appreciation for natural wood that an adult does.

Toys are learning tools, ways of providing stimulation to your child. They help a child begin to develop the eye/hand coordination that will be crucial when she goes to school. Just as babies and young children like adults who respond to them, so they like toys that are responsive—toys that do things. Educational experts call these toys "cause-and-effect" toys. A cause-and-effect toy can be very simple: a rattle that makes a noise when the baby grasps it and shakes it. Or it can be more complicated: a toy that has a little man that pops up when the child presses the right lever. Cause-and-effect toys teach a child that she can make something happen—that she is competent. Cause-and-effect toys with objects that pop up and disappear, like jack-

More Than Child's Play

in-the-boxes, can also begin to teach a child what Piaget called "object permanence." A child understands object permanence when she knows that when she leaves the room the objects in the room won't disappear because she's gone. A child of, say, three months does not have a sense of object permanence. She is totally egocentric, believing that the world does not exist outside the boundaries of her being.

An eight-month-old will search for and find a hidden rattle if he has seen the rattle and knows it exists. For a child of this age, object permanence is a dimly realized concept: the existence of the rattle is tied to the act of finding it. A child who is approaching two can usually find a hidden toy after he's been away from the toy for a full day, indicating that he has some sense of object permanence and knows objects exist apart from himself.

Toys are also primitive problem-solving toys for very young children who are groping to learn problem-solving skills. A child who learns early from his toys that he is effective at making something happen is learning a lesson about self-esteem that will help him when he goes to school or gets his first job. If your child learns early that he can open and shut the doors of a dump truck or make a pull toy travel across the floor, he'll be more likely to feel that—when the time comes—he can do multiplication or write his name. This is Eric Berne's natural child in action, feeling good about himself.

When you buy a cause-and-effect toy, a game or puzzle that's appropriate for your child's age, try not to demonstrate to him how it works. He wants the learning experience of exploring the toy with eyes and hands (and maybe his ears, if the toy makes a sound) and discovering for himself how to make the toy do whatever it's supposed to do. For example, you might buy (or make) a sturdy hands-on hanging mobile or stabile (stationary "mobile") the child can touch as well as look at. When the child pulls one ball down, the other might rise. Your child will learn a lot more from exploring this active mobile than he would from a "don't touch" mobile that hangs passively from the ceiling and is simply pretty to look at.

When you go browsing in toy stores, look for toys that have holes or slots for children to put an object through, or simple puzzle toys with spaces for shapes. You can find toys that expand, allowing the child to stick pieces on a base, take them off, and start all new ones, building a new creation every time.

Stacking toys are also favorites of very young children. Stacking toys can be rings in graduated sizes that fit over a peg, or boxes or bowls in graduated sizes that fit inside each other. Your child will learn about different sizes and spatial relationships by exploring stacking toys with care and concentration.

You don't even need to go out and buy toys to give your youngster a learning experience at home. A clean, empty tin can with no sharp edges and with a plastic lid (the kind coffee comes in) makes a wonderful learning toy for a child who's beginning to explore objects. You can play a peek-a-boo game by putting objects inside the can for the child to find. The can could be a rattle: the toddler can shake the can (with the plastic lid on) to hear the kinds of sounds the objects make when they're inside. The child can use her developing hand muscles to try to pull off the lid or, when the lid is off, to fit it back on (harder).

If you cut a hole in the top of that plastic lid, your child can drop objects through the hole. She will learn that some objects are too big to fit, while some drop easily through the slot. Old metal pots and pans that can be banged with a wooden spoon and sets of stacking (plastic, not glass) mixing bowls make wonderful learning toys for a young child.

Puppets as Teachers

In addition to cause-and-effect toys and toys that stack or nest, young children respond to and learn through simple puppets. A puppet is basically "anything you can bring to life: any inanimate object," notes Mary Jane Fields, a puppeteer and early childhood teacher at Missouri Western State College in St. Joseph, Missouri. Puppets are terrific teachers in the hands of parents, because you and your child can talk and act through puppets.

An inverted Styrofoam punch cup with two fingers punched through the top for "ears" can become a rabbit (add eyes, nose, and mouth with marking pens). The rabbit gains a suit of clothes if you put a napkin over your hand (or let the child do it) before you invert the Styrofoam cup. A half of a peanut shell can be given a face and yarn hair and stuck on a finger.

You can draw animals and people (or cut them out of magazines), back them with cardboard, and glue them onto wooden Popsicle sticks or tongue depressors. An empty oatmeal or cornmeal box with a window cut out on the top portion makes a perfect puppet stage.

How can puppets help your child learn? In her work with very young children, Fields has found that parents can use puppets to:

1) tell a story;
2) teach recognition of feelings and empathy for others;
3) teach ethnic lessons that help a young child value the differences between people; and
4) help the child to change self-defeating behavior (thumb-sucking, for instance).

Puppets work as teaching tools because children are so quick to suspend their disbelief, enter a world of fantasy, and accept a Styrofoam cup as a rabbit. "In today's world, children need to be able to fantasize," says Fields. "I know there's a limit to fantasy, but a little bit helps." Your child will welcome a puppet friend who comes to life occasionally. He will listen to what the puppet has to say. He may work the puppet with his hand himself. And when he becomes older and more verbal, he may talk through the puppet.

Consider Beth, an active three-year-old whose mother had to have an abdominal operation and recover quietly at home for six weeks. Beth had trouble accepting her mother's week in the hospital and her lengthy recovery period. Before her operation, Beth's mother made a mommy puppet from a white athletic tube sock. On one side she sewed eyes, nose, and a happy, smiling mouth. On the other she also sewed on eyes and a nose, but she added a downturned, sad mouth. She tacked on some yarn hair and put a piece of cardboard inside to keep the sock puppet stiff.

When Beth's mother came home, she took the mommy puppet out of the cupboard and put it on her hand. She turned the sad face to Beth and talked through the puppet. "See the sad look on my face, Beth," she said, dipping the puppet's face down. "That's because I'm not feeling very well. I have to rest until my stomach feels much better. Do you think you can help me feel good enough so I'll look like this again?" She turned the puppet's happy face to Beth. Beth was entranced with the puppet.

She touched the two mouths with her fingers and looked at her mother. She had learned a valuable lesson that even young children can learn: that her parent isn't always happy and lively. Beth will be much more likely to respect her mother's feelings and her need for quiet and rest. Would Beth have reacted the same way if her mother had said, "Beth, go away and play by yourself or watch TV. I'm too sick to play with you"?

Toys as Comforters

Toys comfort as well as stimulate and teach. From the time a child is a baby, he needs soft, huggable stuffed animals to squeeze and play with. There is nothing quite like hugging a favorite teddy bear or floppy dog when you are a one-year-old and feeling sick, tired, or frustrated. Huggable toys bring solace. They are a child's size, and so they help the child define his very own personal world. Teddy, the child realizes, does not belong to Mother or Father. Teddy does not belong to a brother, sister, or visiting playmate. Teddy is mine. Teddy stays in my crib or sits on a chair in my room.

A favorite stuffed toy or a security blanket like the one that belongs to Linus, the "Peanuts" cartoon character, is important to a child because she must begin to learn that she can comfort herself when she doesn't feel well. A beloved toy or blanket helps the child nurture herself: develop the inner resources to make herself feel better.

This sense of being able to comfort herself is important, because you won't always be there to pick up your child when she falls, put a band-aid on her scraped knee, or wipe the tears from her cheek. Although a blanket or stuffed toy cannot guarantee mental health, studies of psychopathic individuals by Connecticut psychiatrist Paul C. Horton have actually shown that many, when young, lacked a solacing object such as a teddy bear. In older people, a beloved pet often replaces the teddy bear for solace.

Parental Play Styles

Research has shown that how a parent plays with a child often differs according to sex. In general, fathers tend to play with their babies in a generally zippier, more rollicking and altogether physical way than their spouses. Mothers, on the other hand, tend to hold and talk to their children, and to give them toys to play with. Both styles of play are valuable to the child. The father's physical play helps the child develop coordination and a sense of spatial relations, while the mother's play style nurtures concentration and verbal skills.

A mother who jumps up and screams, "You're going to drop the baby!" when the father swings his child in the air will not only discourage the baby's physical development and instill him with fear, but will also discourage her husband from playing with his baby in his own natural way.

Whether you are a mother or a father, you can help to foster your child's natural inner love of play by creating an atmosphere at home that nurtures the concept of play. For play to be really play, it must take place in a relaxed, casual setting.

Do you provide your child with a place where the rules get shelved, a room where it's perfectly O.K. to climb on the furniture, rearrange things, turn a chair upside down so it can become a tent or a cave? Do you have a true playroom, a room where learning through play is valued, approved of, supported? It doesn't have to be big, and it doesn't have to have fancy equipment or toys. It should have bright colors, since even very young babies can respond to bright blues, yellows, and reds.

And don't neglect the outdoors when you're thinking of play spaces. "The design of our outdoor play rooms should reflect the same concern for the use of color, form, texture and diversity that we insist upon in the design of indoor spaces," in the words of early childhood professor Steen B. Esbensen, executive director of the Canadian Society for the Study of Education. If you don't have a yard of your own, make sure your apartment complex does, or that there's a park with a playground nearby. In Denmark, notes Esbensen, a national policy on children's play spaces is drafted right into the building code.

Toy Lending Libraries

To expand your child's toy learning experiences without spending a lot of money, you might want to take a cue from Swedish educators and establish a circulating toy library with parents of young children in your neighborhood.

The idea of an educational toy lending library was born in 1963 in Stockholm as a way to help handicapped children to improve their physical and mental abilities. It was a cooperative effort between parents and early childhood teachers. In Sweden there are now more than sixty nonprofit toy lending libraries called "lekoteks" (*lek* is the Swedish word for play, and *tek* is the Greek word for library). Elizabeth Larm, president of the Swedish Lekotek Association, believes children should start active learning as babies, and that lekoteks can help. Lekoteks have been adapted in more than thirty other countries.

In January 1981, the first American lekotek opened in Evanston, Illinois. It was organized by Sarah de Vincentis, a special education teacher who was trained by lekotek teachers in Sweden to help select toys for handicapped or retarded children with special learning needs. "Appropriate toys are children's tools," notes De Vincentis, who now serves as executive director of the Evanston Lekotek.

She is a strong supporter of parents using lekoteks to help their children learn and grow. "Lekotek encourages parents to believe in themselves," she says.

While lekoteks are for children with special needs—mental retardation, cerebral palsy, autism, and deafness—the idea of an educational toy lending library can be adapted for normal children in virtually any neighborhood. Perhaps your local library already sponsors a section that lends toys. If not, you might start an informal toy lending program in your own neighborhood. Originally, everyone who wants to participate might contribute one teaching toy (it helps if the children are close in age); the toys could be added as more parents join, or the original group of parents might purchase more.

In choosing toys for a neighborhood lekotek, remember that the whole idea is to have an educational toy lending library. Choose toys that teach.

The Toy Dilemma

Many American educators—including Sarah de Vincentis—don't think much of the majority of mass-produced American toys when it comes to their ability to help children learn. She terms the U.S. toy industry "fickle and faddish," qualities which she attributes to the influence of heavy television advertising to a young and captive audience. "There is a commercialization of toys here that is not true in Europe," she says. "Toys in Europe are very classically designed."

The truth is that too many toys break. Too many have little moving parts that get lost or fall off (or, far worse, swallowed). Too many are faddishly tied to the latest movie or television ad, and have value only because they're imitative of what a child sees on the screen. The 1983 pre-Christmas stampede by parents to buy the Cabbage Patch dolls was a direct result of a very clever television advertising campaign, not the result of a child's innate desire to have a Cabbage Patch doll.

If you've shopped in a store that carries European toys, you've already noticed that many tend to be made of natural materials such as wood, or sturdy, brightly colored plastic. These toys are durable, and some last long enough to be handed down to your children's children.

In 1976, former teacher and former day-care director Lane Nemeth, the mother of a young daughter, became frustrated by the lack of high-quality educational toys available to parents of young children in this country. As an educator, she had bought and taught with hundreds of fine educational toys available in specialized lines. But she could not buy them as a consumer. Nemeth launched Discovery Toys, a California-based company that orders handpicked educational toys from around the world (including high-quality toys from this country).

Discovery Toys trains women (many of whom are former teachers) to go into homes and demonstrate for mothers which toys are good learning tools for which age ranges and abilities. The mothers can handle the toys and talk to the Discovery Toys visitor about their children's needs and play styles. The toys, available for sale, have been tested by Discovery Toys' employees before being included in the catalog.

Discovery Toys is a mushrooming, profit-making business. In February 1982 Lane Nemeth was cited in the business magazine *Inc.* as a successful small-business entrepreneur sought by investment companies who want a piece of Discovery Toys. But Nemeth sees her business as more than a profit sheet. She sees it as a way to demonstrate for parents what educational toys can do for their children, and to give them a chance to buy the tools of learning. Many of the toys Nemeth buys for her warehouses in Benicia, California, are from Denmark, Great Britain, and West Germany. She travels throughout the United States and Europe, looking at thousands of toys before selecting the ones for her catalog.

Your Ideas about Play

Before trying to plan play experiences or buy toys for your child, it's a good idea to examine your own feelings about play so you know what kind of signals you're sending your child. Do you inadvertently transmit the message that play is "frivolous" or "wrong"? (Some of us are so steeped in the American work ethic that we tend to frown on the whole idea of play, and it may rub off on our children.) Or do you value play and take care to make time in your day for your child's playtime? Consider the following scenes:

SCENE ONE

Jeff, age two, comes up to his mother, who is in the middle of putting clothes in the washer. He tries to hand her a metal dump truck. Jeff's mother, annoyed and trying to finish the laundry, pushes the dump truck away and frowns. Jeff, getting the message that his mother doesn't think it's as important to play with him as it is to do laundry, looks puzzled. Then, being a bright and active two-year-old, Jeff reacts with anger. He's annoyed that his mother won't come and play, so he starts to yell and throws the truck on the floor. His mother, who

More Than Child's Play

has never looked away from the laundry basket and the washer, raises her voice. "I'm busy!" she says in a loud, angry tone. "Go away and play by yourself!"

Scene Two

Bobby, also two, comes up to his mother, who is sweeping the kitchen floor. He hands her his stuffed elephant. Bobby's mother stops sweeping, stands the broom against the wall, and accepts the elephant, which she hugs. "Oh, thank you, Bobby," she says. "Is Babar coming to visit me?" Bobby claps his hands and laughs. "Maybe Babar would like to help me sweep," she continues. She takes the elephant and places the broom between the animal's front legs, putting her hands around the elephant. She continues to sweep, with the elephant "helping."

Bobby, delighted that he and his favorite stuffed animal have been drawn into his mother's activity, follows her around, watching the elephant "sweep." He picks up a piece of paper towel on the floor and hands it to her, helping clean up. She thanks him. Eventually Bobby raises his arms up for the elephant. The mother hugs him again and gives him back to Bobby. "Bye, bye, Babar," she says, waving. Bobby toddles off happily with the elephant.

Which child will be more likely to learn to play independently and develop a sense of concentration, motivation, and the ability to stick with something? Not Jeff, who is learning to fly into a rage when his mother won't drop everything and come play. Bobby, on the other hand, has learned that his mother considers his play and his playmate (Babar) important enough to stop sweeping briefly and draw him and his elephant into what she is doing in a playful way.

In the next chapters, we'll go beyond the phenomenon of free play to look at how you can turn your home, which is your child's first school, into an environment where learning takes place naturally and joyfully.

Five Learning Toys You Already Own

Tired of spending lots of money on learning toys you're not sure your child will really like? Look around the house for these learning toys you probably already have on hand:

1. A set of plastic mixing bowls in graduated sizes that stack. Your child will learn about size and order as he unstacks the bowls and then puts the stack back together. He'll see that a large bowl just can't fit inside a smaller bowl.

2. A clean empty coffee can with a plastic lid. Put objects of various sizes, shapes, and weights in the can and let your child shake it. She'll learn to identify subtle differences in sounds (a spool of thread makes a different sound from a stainless steel spoon), and she'll learn—when she picks up the can—that certain objects are heavier than others.

3. A cotton tube sock for a hand puppet. Sew on two buttons for eyes, stick on a nose and mouth, and tack on some yarn hair. Let the puppet "talk" to your child.

4. Empty wooden thread spools (large and small). They're fun to stack; little fingers will gain dexterity as your child sees how high the stack will go before it tumbles over.

Your child will also learn that the stacking works better if the large spools are on the bottom.

5. A half of a peanut shell for a finger puppet. Draw on a nose, mouth, and eyes with a felt-tipped pen. Let your child "wear" the puppet on his finger, or you can put the peanut puppet on your own finger.

6. Tell Me a Story

> The fairy tale is the primer from which the child learns to read his mind in the language of images, the only language which permits understanding before intellectual maturity has been achieved. The child needs to be exposed to this language, and must learn to be responsive to it, if he is to become master of his soul.
>
> —Bruno Bettelheim, *The Uses of Enchantment*

A bright, inquisitive preschooler is a natural for storytelling. Even before he can really talk—when he is a toddler between the ages of one and two—he will respond creatively to your own storytelling and to simple picture books with brightly colored drawings of people and animals. When he is between two and three, your child will delight in telling you his own original stories.

What is a story? Why does a bright, curious child respond so readily to storytelling? How can you use this natural love of stories to help your child learn? Before men and women learned to draw pictures on a rough stone cave wall or put words on papyrus, there were stories. They were tales based on real adventures—fighting an enemy tribesman or hunting a buffalo—or tall tales concocted by a master raconteur.

The Dynamic Art

Storytelling, as opposed to viewing a movie or watching a television sitcom, is dynamic, intimate, a shared experience between storyteller and listener. This intimacy, this active engagement, is what so enchants your child. It isn't just the facts of the tale he responds to—what happend to and to whom—but the cadence and inflection of your voice, the pauses, the expression in your eyes. Your child is above all interested in you, and what you feel and believe in. A movie or television program never stops, but you can stop in the middle of a story, pause, repeat something for emphasis, go back and remind your child of something that happened in the beginning. You can adjust the pace of the story to your child's attention span, slowing down when you want to and speeding up when you wish.

Your involvement in the story you're telling teaches a child as much as the content of the story itself. Stories with action, stories with a moral, stories alive with the joy of human relationships—these are all enriched by your facial expressions, tone of voice, even your body gestures, such as a shrug of the shoulders or a turn of your head. Your child is smart enough to pick up on these body language cues from you, and to put them together with the words he's hearing to form a creative experience.

As you read a simple story to your young child, you'll want to do far more than just read the words; you'll want to embellish or even leave out parts according to your child's reactions. For a toddler, a story should be very short, because her attention span is short. Older preschoolers and children in the first grades of school can be introduced to fairy tales. Fairy tales, points out child psychologist Bruno Bettelheim, help a child understand herself better. They shouldn't be read word for word, belabored or "explained," he notes, because through the telling and retelling the child will draw her own conclusions about heroes and cowards, evil and kindness. "Slavishly sticking to the way a fairy story is printed robs it of much of its value," he points out. "The telling of a story to a child, to be most effective, has to be an interpersonal event, shaped by those who participate in it."

Before your child can reason in the adult sense, you can help him learn about life in the language he understands, what Bettelheim calls "the language of images."

Capturing Your Child's World

What kind of stories are best for a young child? Many parents, after a trip to the local library or bookstore, are overwhelmed by the variety of books available for reading to small children. When he is a toddler, a child responds best to books with pictures of familiar pets and people and of household objects such as chairs and dishes because they are part of his own world. When he is older he will relate more readily to exotic tales of faraway places and strange heroes with even stranger names.

It's revealing to see the kinds of books selected for preschoolers by the Child Study Children's Book Committee at the Bank Street College of Education in New York. The committee is a group of parents, teachers, librarians, writers, and illustrators who are intensely interested in and concerned about the quality of books for children. The committee reviewed 2,000 books published for children in 1982 to select 400 for its 1983 annotated list of recommended titles.

In the age group three, four, and five (the youngest age category the committee designated), members picked books that primarily show a young child's daily experiences, not Arabian Nights extravaganzas that bear little relationship to real life. Three of the books selected are alphabet books with pictures that depict familiar objects and daily activities that go with letters of the alphabet.

Another selected story, called *Chuckie,* is a picture book

about accepting a new baby in the family, while *Clean Enough* is a picture book about having fun in the bath. *Peter Spier's Rain* is a wordless picture book showing that rainy days can be fun, not sad. *Hello Kitty Sleeps Over* is a comforting story about spending the night with grandparents, which can be an unsettling new experience for even the most adventuresome preschoolers. All these books selected by the committee are about real events or experience; they attempt to make the bright child's world more understandable and vivid to him.

Creative Storyboards

But you don't even need books to tell your young child a story. All you really need is your own imagination and your child's. Why not make a set of storytelling cards, which can be used in a vast number of combinations according to your whim and your child's tastes of the moment? Here's how it works. You simply cut pictures of people, animals, houses, and trees out of magazines. Paste the pictures on unlined index cards or on pieces of cardboard (shirt cardboard from the laundry works fine) cut to the same size. The cardboard backing will keep the storyboards from getting torn and allow you to reuse them in various combinations.

You might start with ten or twenty story cards, adding more as you go along and as your child picks out pictures he likes in magazines. Once he gets the hang of storyboards, he'll probably start pointing to pictures he likes. When storytelling time comes, first think of a simple story line and then pick out the pictures on the storyboards that most nearly illustrate your plot. Or just shuffle the story-

Tell Me a Story

boards in a random order and make up a story as you go along, according to the way the images happen to come up on cards you select. As you tell the story, embellishing and adding here and there, show a storyboard picture that helps you get across the point you're making.

For instance, suppose you want to tell a story about a child going to select a pet and bringing it home. (Maybe your own child is getting a pet, and you want to impress on him that the pet needs to be cared for with food, water, brushing, and shots from the veterinarian.)

You can start with a picture of a small boy or girl, show a picture of his or her house, show a picture of a car (for going to the animal shelter or pet store), and then show a picture of the puppy or kitten the child selects. You can finish the story by showing a picture of the inside of a house and pointing to the picture of the pet, explaining that the pet has come to stay and is now a member of the family. There are all sorts of ways you can add to the story. Cut out pictures of dog or cat food, mount them on cardboard, and use them to explain that young pets, like children, need good food to grow up strong and healthy.

You can let your child help you choose pictures for the growing storyboard collection. Your child will come to value the collection of pictures for storyboards because he will associate them with the magic time you share together. He will look forward to having you bring the collection out and select exactly the cards you want to use for the special story you want to tell.

Can stories really help your bright, inquisitive youngster learn? Absolutely. Your child can learn about how-to things, like feeding pets. Your child can learn about feelings: that people feel sad sometimes, angry sometimes, and sometimes joyous.

Learning to Share

As we've seen, young children are naturally very egocentric; they have to be to survive. That's their protection against being forgotten or ignored, their way of ensuring they'll be fed, hugged, clothed, washed, played with, and included in their parents' lives. As a baby, your child is a bundle of wants and needs, a new little "I" making her presence and her wishes known at every waking moment. As she grows older, she can begin to comprehend that other people have needs and feelings, too. She can begin to see the glimmer of other viewpoints than her own.

Florida educators Suzanne Lowell Krogh and Linda Leonard Lamme point out that stories can help even preschoolers begin to learn the difficult and unnatural concept of sharing—an abstract idea that's foreign to the egocentric child—by putting the act of sharing into a more concrete setting. Your child, by actively listening to a story, can begin to get a sense of what it's like to step into the shoes of someone else for a little while. He can begin to understand and appreciate someone else's point of view, a very difficult task for a child. Awareness of others' feelings is an extremely tough idea for a child to grasp; indeed, there are some adults who are hopeless at it. But this awareness should begin in the early years, and stories are the perfect way to introduce it.

Animal characters in stories can help in this important discovery process. For example, Krogh and Lamme cite the book *Angus and the Cat,* a story about two animals written for preschoolers. In this book Angus, a self-centered dog, doesn't want to share a patch of sunlight with a cat. But then the cat runs away and Angus has the patch of sunlight all to himself. Instead of being happy, he realizes that he misses the cat's company. He realizes that the cat was really his friend and he should have been more willing to share the patch of sunlight. In order to get the cat to come back and share his sunlight, Angus shares a saucer of milk with his feline friend.

Of course, no story is going to transform a basically egocentric child into an altruistic sharer overnight, but a sensitively told story can help a child begin to see that other people have needs, wants, and feelings, too. You can use your own storyboards to make up a story about sharing at home, maybe based on a real experience your child has had with a friend or an older sister or brother.

New research from the National Institute of Mental Health and Chestnut Lodge in Rockville, Maryland, indicates that children under two, although basically self-centered, are capable of altruism and empathy. The concern about others demonstrated by altruistic behavior is just beginning between the ages of twelve and fifteen months, note researchers Carolyn Zahn-Waxler, Marian Radke-Yarrow, and Robert King. During this stage, a child will typically pat or touch someone who is crying or obviously in distress. Not surprisingly, the children who showed the most concern for others in studies done by the three researchers had mothers who were themselves caring and full of empathy. These children were extremely sensitive to other people's bad moods, sorrow, and conflicts. Through listening to stories that reinforce the feelings of others, a sensitive child is learning how to be a caring and altruisitic human being.

Your Child as Storyteller

So far, we've talked about your telling stories to your child. But preschoolers, when you encourage them, will tell their own original, vivid stories with great enthusiasm. The stories may be only two or three sentences long, but they are creative stories all the same.

In 1963, Tufts University educator Evelyn Goodenough Pitcher and her Yale University co-author, Ernst Prelinger, published a collection of original stories told by 137 children, about half from boys and half from girls. The children were all preschoolers or kindergarteners, and some were as young as two. Pitcher gathered the stories from 1955 to 1958, mostly during regular sessions of nursery school or kindergarten in the area around New Haven, Connecticut. In all, Pitcher and Prelinger collected 360 stories (most children contributed several stories).

A glance at the stories of the youngest children reveals bright, curious, aware minds making remarkably sound sense of a confusing world. Some of the stories Pitcher gathered were amazingly detailed for a child just learning to express himself in the language adults use. Consider this story from a boy aged two years, ten months:

"I hurt my leg and I tell my mommy. I got a scratch and she put Band-Aid on it. And I put Band-Aid on my hand. And I went on a good truck ride. I fall down in the truck, and the car run over me. And I hurt myself in the street, and it was a bone. I got in the truck and the man shut the door so I won't fall out the truck. And then I bumped my head in the truck. Then I ride in the airplane and go to my grandpa."

This little boy, not yet three, is able to express a wide range of very complicated concepts: getting hurt on not one but two different levels of severity (a "scratch" and a "bone"); not one but three kinds of transportation (a truck, a car, an airplane); the sophisticated concept of physical safety (a man shuts the door of the truck so the little boy won't fall out); and the notion of long distances (going by

Tell Me a Story

air to see his grandfather, who lives far away). When analyzed, this story seems amazingly complex for a child under three—until you realize that all bright, curious children in tune with their environment are capable of making such perceptive observations if they're encouraged to do so.

Consider another story, this one told by a little girl two years and nine months old:

"The baby cried. The mommy picked it up. The mommy put it back to bed. The baby looked at the little flowers. She took a string and fussed with it. She had slippers on. She got sick. The mommy had to feed her. She got a toy horse. An airplane came around the sky. Her daddy came. She ate her supper. She went to sleep."

In this story, a child not yet three shows tremendous powers of observation, noting exactly what the baby (probably her little sister) wore (slippers), did (looked at small flowers and "fussed" with string), was given as a gift (a toy horse) and how she spent her time (got sick, ate her supper, went to sleep). She notices small details about another human being, a baby, and observes an airplane flying over the house.

Pitcher coaxed and encouraged her young friends to tell her original stories. She made them feel that their creative stories mattered. She didn't give up on the shy ones. She would take a child aside into a quiet corner of the classroom and make friends. If a child declined to tell an original story, she'd say, "Not today, but perhaps another day you will tell me a story." If a child seemed to get stuck in the middle of a story, she'd ask enthusiastically, "What happened next?"

Coaxing an original story from your preschool child will give you an intriguing peek into the child's richly creative imagination. If your preschool child starts retelling a fairy story or nursery rhyme, such as "The Three Bears," or retelling a show she saw on TV, gently say something like "I'd like to hear your very own story, one you make up all by yourself."

You might want to establish a routine of shared storytelling both you and your child can look forward to. Perhaps four nights a week you'll read a bedtime story to your child or make up a fresh one using your storyboards. The other three nights, encourage your child to tell you a story. Maybe she'd like to use some of the storyboards herself. Maybe you'd like to cut out more pictures for mounting as the seasons come and go to help your child develop a concept of passing time: a snow scene, a Christmas tree, the daffodils of spring, an ocean beach for summer.

Learning Right from Wrong

We've seen that storytelling can help your child start to develop a sense of sharing and the ability to see events from someone else's viewpoint. Storytelling can also help develop a sense of right and wrong, the moral sense Piaget said must be nurtured in young children if they are to grow into responsible adults.

In analyzing the 360 stories contributed by the 137 children in their study, Pitcher and Prelinger found that there was little morality in the sense of taking personal responsibility in the youngest children's stories. The concepts of taking personal responsibility for actions—good or bad— and determining the possible consequences of an action ahead of time are too sophisticated for most preschoolers. Instead, the stories express what Piaget termed the "morality of constraint": a concept based on what parents *say* is good or bad. The moral horizon of the two-year-old is limited to activities close to the domestic world of home:

badness means pushing, scratching, crying. Only one two-year-old actually used the term "good" in a story.

The stories of three-year-olds, on the other hand, showed a greater awareness of aggressive actions as "badness"—especially actions that hurt other people. For instance, in one story a bad bear climbs into a good bear's bed; in another, parents get a new baby bear who is "good." The stories also showed that three-year-olds can begin to develop the important but complicated notion that badness and goodness can exist in the same person. In one story a child describes a little girl called Bobbie as "sometimes good, sometimes bad."

Studies by Zahn-Waxler, Radke-Yarrow, and King indicate that as a child goes into her second year of life, she starts to develop a conscience. In other words, as the child is learning to be more caring toward others, she is also learning that she can hurt others. This is the beginning of guilt. Children in the researchers' studies were likely to see themselves as the cause of injuries, even though they weren't necessarily anywhere near when an accident happened. Thus a child feeling the first guilt pangs might say, "Did I hurt you, Mommy?" even when she clearly wasn't the cause of her mother's harm. Through examining issues of right and wrong in simple terms in stories on her level, a child can begin to come to terms with conscience and guilt.

Your child's most creative ideas come from the natural-child ego state named by Eric Berne, the personal part of your child that most needs nurturing as he grows up in a rigidly ordered world where people are expected to behave in a certain way according to preset rules. Original storytelling helps your child order his world and express his feelings and ideas without totally ruining the creative aspects of that nonlinear, free-association thinking process so natural to any bright child. Original stories have a beginning and an end. But they have no set patterns your child must live by in the telling: he is allowed, encouraged to create his own pattern.

A Sense of Fantasy

As your child grows older and is asked to meet expectations and set goals, that intensely creative free-association part of him can get drowned in a sea of musts and shoulds. Helping your child keep a sense of fantasy alive becomes urgently important: this is the part of her that may give birth to a symphony, a poem, a new scientific explanation of why normal cells become cancerous, a cathedral, a movie, or a novel.

Bettelheim believes—and he is certainly right—that many parents tend to be put off by fairy tales and fantasy. They fear a child may come to believe in "magic," may not learn to cope with "reality," may live only in daydreams and withdraw from the world of real people, objects, and events. But exactly the opposite is true. In fact, Bettelheim notes, a sense of fantasy frees the mind from narrow, confining daydreams: ". . . free-floating fantasy, which contains in imaginary form a wide variety of issues also encountered in reality, provides the ego with an abundance of material to work with. This rich and variegated fantasy life is provided to the child by fairy stories, which can help prevent his imagination from getting stuck within the narrow confines of a few anxious or wish-fulfilling daydreams circling around a few narrow preoccupations."

Fantasy as expressed in storytelling is one way a child

comes to understand himself and his world. It's the child's equivalent of brainstorming, a kind of freewheeling creative thinking process. To remove fantasy—again in the words of Bettelheim, to "offer a child rational thought as his major instrument for sorting out his feelings and understanding the world"—will only confuse him.

Fantasy, verbal lessons, moral growth: storytelling is all of these. And finally it is also a quiet time of shared intimacy for you and your child. There is nothing quite so satisfying as telling your story to someone who is just dying to hear it and who hangs on every word. There is nothing quite so compelling as hearing an original story—even if it is only two sentences long—from a child who has made it up himself by observing his world. Your child, the natural storyteller and story listener, deserves nothing less than a chance to be both.

Once Upon a Time: Reading Readiness

In addition to being fun and helping your child cope with her world, storytelling helps to prepare the child for reading. Long before he is ready to really read a book, he is learning about sounds, make-believe characters in pictures, the structure of stories (they have a beginning, middle, and end), words, and letters. He is learning how to sit quietly and listen, or how to communicate his own original stories.

The more familiar and comfortable your child is with words and with books—what they look like, what they feel like to the touch—the readier your child will be to learn to read. Reading readiness is something all parents can help their children achieve by valuing stories and storytelling at home. To help your child get ready for reading, try these practical suggestions based on research by the National Association for the Education of Young Children.

For Infants

1. Talk to your baby—during play, while giving your infant a bath, while feeding her, while changing diapers. Speak slowly and distinctly.

2. Sing to your baby—songs that make you happy, not necessarily children's songs.

3. Prop up a sturdy cardboard picture book in the crib or on the floor for a two- to four-month-old (cloth books are too floppy to stand). Your baby won't know this is a book, in the sense of something to read, but will become familiar with what a book looks like and how to handle it as an object that's part of her world (gently take the book out of the baby's mouth if it ends up as something to chew on).

4. For an older baby, point to a specific picture in the book and name it. Repeat the name. Do this for a number of the pictures in the book, and repeat this procedure so the child begins to get used to associating a word with a specific picture.

5. When the baby is old enough to ride in the seat of a grocery cart, take him along with you when you shop and give him small boxes of raisins or animal crackers to hold. Talk about what is in the boxes, making up stories about how the raisins or animals get into the boxes.

6. At about one year of age, your child will probably begin to notice letters on blocks. Talk about the letters, repeating their sounds.

For Toddlers and Preschoolers

1. Read to your child before she goes to bed, and during the day at a special story time you have established.

Tell Me a Story

Don't be discouraged or bored when she asks for the same favorite book over and over again. Children love repetition.

2. Keep magnetic letters on your refrigerator door. Let your child touch them, and become familiar with what letters look like.

3. Take your child to the library and visit the children's room. Let him look at and handle the books on the shelves.

4. Read posters and large picture displays aloud so the child can associate the pictures with the words.

5. Encourage the child to draw thank-you notes in pictures for birthday and Christmas presents with crayons.

6. Pause while reading and encourage your child to tell you what happens next in a familiar story—"What did the dog do then?" Add some new books to your child's collection, but continue to read old favorites because it will reinforce the child's feeling that books are old friends.

7. Keep a favorite book in your purse for those draggy times when you have to wait with your child at the doctor's office or another place where you have an appointment.

Recommended Books for Ages Three, Four, and Five

(1982 books selected by the Child Study Children's Book Committee at Bank Street College of Education in New York)

1. *Aaron Awoke: An Alphabet Story,* by Marilee Robin Burton. Harper & Row, $8.95. A little boy goes through his daily routine in pictures, and also goes through the alphabet.

2. *A, B, See!* by Tana Hoban. Greenwillow Books, $8.50. Pictures of familiar objects help children identify the letters of the alphabet.

3. *Airport,* written and illustrated by Byron Barton. Thomas Y. Crowell, $9.95. Large, bright pictures show the preparation for passengers, luggage, and takeoff of a plane in an airport.

4. *Ben's ABC Day,* by Terry Burger with photos by Alice Kandell. Lothrop, Lee, & Shepard, $9.50. Photographs of daily activities that represent the letters of the alphabet.

5. *Bread and Honey,* written and illustrated by Frank Asch. Parents Magazine, $5.95. In this story for the very young, a small bear's portrait of his mother goes through many changes.

6. *Chuckie,* written and illustrated by Nicki Weiss. Greenwillow Books, $8.00. This is a picture story about accepting a new baby in the family.

7. *Clean Enough,* written and illustrated by Kevin Henkes. Greenwillow Books, $8.50. A book about having fun in the bath.

8. *The First Words Picture Book,* by Bill Gillham with photos by Sam Grainger. Coward, McCann & Geoghegan, $7.95. A book for a child who has just turned three and is becoming comfortable with words.

9. *Hello Kitty Sleeps Over,* written by Robin Harris and illustrated by J. M. L. Gray. Random House, $3.50. A reassuring tale about staying overnight with grandparents.

10. *How My Garden Grew* and *Sick in Bed,* written and illustrated by Anne and Harlow Rockwell. Macmillan, $6.95. Two stories about two everyday experiences: gardening and recovering in bed.

11. *Kate's Box, Kate's Car, Kate's Quilt, Kate's Snowman,* written and illustrated by Kay Chorao. E. P. Dutton, $3.95 each. Four small books tell the story of an elephant child and her family.

12. *Let's Play,* written and illustrated by Satomi Ichi-

Tell Me a Story

kawa. Philomel Books, $9.99. A book with pictures that tell their own stories.

13. *Moonlight,* written and illustrated by Jan Ormerod. Lothrop, Lee, & Shepard, $9.50. A story without words about the bedtime of a little girl.

14. *My Melody's New Bike,* written by Robin Harris and illustrated by Carolyn Bracken. Random House, $3.50. A story about Melody's birthday.

15. *1 Hunter,* written and illustrated by Pat Hutchins. Greenwillow Books, $9.50. A counting book.

16. *Owly,* written by Mike Thaler, and illustrated by David Wiesner. Harper & Row, $9.50. Depicts a child's curiosity about the world and a mother satisfying that curiosity.

17. *Paddy Goes Traveling,* written and illustrated by John S. Goodall. Atheneum, $6.95. The pig Paddy Pork has sea and land adventures in pictures.

18. *Peter Spier's Rain,* written and illustrated by Peter Spier. Doubleday, $10.95. A wordless picture book about experiences that can make rainy days fun.

19. *The Sun's Asleep Behind the Hill,* written by Mirra Ginsburg and illustrated by Paul O. Zelinsky. Greenwillow Books, $9.50. The world gets sleepy as the child is lulled to sleep with words and pictures.

20. *When You Were a Baby,* written and illustrated by Ann Jonas. Greenwillow Books, $9.50. Pictures of familiar objects in a child's world with brief text.

21. *Wilberforce Goes on a Picnic,* written and illustrated by Margaret Gordon. William Morrow & Company, $9.50. A young bear and his grandparents enjoy an outdoor adventure.

NOTE: Comments on these books are adapted from the notations of the Child Study Children's Book Committee.

In addition to the books listed above, the following book is recommended by educators because it helps a young child learn about sharing;

Angus and the Cat, by Marjorie Flack. Doubleday, 1971. The dog Angus resents having to share his patch of sunlight with a cat until the cat runs away and Angus finds out he misses its company. In order to get the cat back, Angus shares a dish of milk.

7. Your Home as a Creative School

> By whatever name one calls it, genuine creativity is characterized by an intensity of awareness, a heightened consciousness.
>
> —ROLLO MAY, *The Courage to Create*

A child is a small bundle of intensely creative energy, a dynamo with unique abilities and a unique vision of the world. That's important to keep in mind when your child doesn't conform—do things in the nice, neat way society deems appropriate. Of course, not every child will grow up to be a Van Gogh or a Beethoven. But recognizing that your child is, in fact, highly creative by nature is the first step in learning to spot and nurture creativity.

If you have an older child, you've probably noticed how that child's drawings started out free and individualistic, with an almost magical quality that defied neat little categories. What your child was doing was creating beautiful personal fantasies with crayons. Green hair, blue horses, purple trees—all were possible.

Then, as your child went to school and progressed through first grade and the higher elementary grades, your child's drawing probably became tighter, more cramped, neater, and more ordinary. Certainly the drawings change partly because the child is exercising increased coordination and hand/eye skills. But the spontaneity and the fantasy may be lost, because of an overly controlling parent or teacher. The pressure to get a grade or some kind of recognition from the teacher only makes greater the newly realized need to restrain personal creativity.

Nurturing Creative Thought

As a parent you can do a great deal in the early years to ensure that your child will develop his creativity fully. A sense of personal creativity will help your child preserve his uniqueness in a world that all too often tends to honor the norm, rather than the unusually talented or the just plain different. Many people who grew up to be recognized as creative geniuses were "different" as children.

To understand how to help your child nurture and preserve her personal creativity, it's important to understand how she thinks. And that's different from the way you think. Adult thinking is often described as linear—a straight line. We have a problem to solve—for example, addressing and mailing our holiday cards. We make a list, probably in alphabetical order for future reference. We address the cards according to information in a source book, the phone directory, an office list, or addresses in an address book. We address each envelope, sign the cards, stuff the envelopes, put a stamp on each envelope, and drop the cards at the post office.

Where did we learn this prosaic series of steps? It's culturally ingrained in us from an early age. Society rewards goal-oriented behavior—accomplishing a task or producing something—as no other human activity. When a child learns the sequence of steps in getting dressed himself, it takes the burden off you. You're delighted, and you praise him. Later in the classroom, the child will be rewarded by his teacher for learning an arbitrary list of letters so he can write, and an arbitrary list of numbers so he can add and subtract. Where will all this get him? To a stage where he can later fill out tax returns and achieve success on the job.

But some personal creativity may be sacrificed in the process.

Babies as Creative Thinkers

As babies, however, we all start out not as linear thinkers, but as champion nonlinear thinkers. A baby's thought has no causality, no sequence, no logical time or space; it occurs as a kind of free-floating mental experience. This nonlinear thinking is highly individualistic and creative, and depends on the personal experiences of the infant and the toddler. It's filled with internal desires for comfort: to be fed, held, changed when wet. As Piaget put it, for a healthy, well-cared-for baby, reality coincides with desire. Although toddlers develop a primitive sense of object permanence, up until the age of about three no world really exists in the child's mind beyond his own physical experience of it, from minute to minute.

What's fascinating about the nonlinear thought patterns of a bright, healthy child is that in recent years researchers have discovered that a child's nonlinear thinking has a lot in common with the thought patterns of creative adults. The right hemisphere of the brain is most closely in touch with the most powerful images and feelings in our minds, and it's the right hemisphere that seems most involved in nonlinear thinking. The right part of the brain works best at an unconscious level, often making enormous and unpredictable leaps of thought.

Psychologist Rollo May, one of the few thinkers who has attempted to define creativity, has described the creative experience as "bursts" of ideas, an intense encounter that demands total absorption. This intensity, he said, characterizes the state of the artist or scientist when creating—

and the child in free play. This intensity of awareness "is not necessarily connected with conscious purpose or willing," May has pointed out. "It may occur in reverie or in dreams, or from so-called unconscious levels." Thinking during these periods of intensity is often free-floating and nonlinear; it may appear to have no particular direction and no specific purpose.

From the very beginning of his life, an infant is flooded with a sea of vivid images and sensations, both from within himself and from outside (even though he can't really distinguish between the two). Sounds, pictures, and feelings hook themselves together in fantastic combinations. As a child grows older, he may attempt to control, shape, and express his individual world of creative experience in drawings, music, or building with blocks. At that point, he will endow the creative experience with purpose. "Purpose involves all levels of experience," May has written. "We cannot *will* to have insights. We cannot *will* creativity. But we can *will* to give ourselves to the encounter with intensity of dedication and commitment. The deeper aspects of awareness are activated to the extent that the person is committed to the encounter." When a child or an adult artist gives purpose to his creative bursts of ideas—bursts that occur in a random and nonlinear way—he is giving his creativity form and shape.

The Creative Parent

You've probably already observed children's creative nonlinear thinking when they play with blocks, for example. Most parents, with their ingrained linear thinking, can't help showing the children the "proper" way to arrange blocks. The largest go on the bottom, the medium-sized ones next, and so forth, until the smallest blocks are on top. While we all need to learn to organize and categorize the world around us, the skill of being able to arrange blocks progressively according to size isn't creative; it's simply rote knowledge. A child, using her own natural creativity, will set the blocks up in any way that pleases her—without regard for the "proper" way to do it. And that's exactly the way it should be.

Very few researchers other than Rollo May have studied the phenomenon of personal creativity in children or adults, although many have studied intelligence. Therefore, we don't know a lot about the creative process or how to nurture and preserve it. We do know it's highly valuable and to be cherished above all other qualities: personal creativity is the special gift a child brings to the world. Creativity, not conformity, has brought us our finest examples of art, architecture, poetry, film, music, and scientific theory.

How do you nurture your child's personal creativity at home? First, become aware that a child's physical environment has a lot to do with fostering creative thinking. University of California (Berkeley) psychologist Donald W. MacKinnon, one of the few researchers who has studied creativity, notes that long ago Hippocrates, the father of medicine (c. 460–377 B.C.), recognized that our physical environment influences human personality. Hippocrates talked of "airs, waters, and places" as directly contributing to differences among people.

Today, rightly or wrongly, we often use stereotypes about geography to explain differences in national personalities. People from Scotland are supposed to be somewhat dour, gruff, and stingy; they live in a cold, barren land. New England Yankees, who live among jagged rocks and driving snow, are also supposed to be dour and strong-willed. Italians are thought of as warm, rollicking, and outgoing—a reflection of their warm, sunny climate.

It's certainly true that, as MacKinnon puts it, "Some environments barely sustain human life to say nothing about fostering creative thought and action." And, he points out, no Pulitzer Prize-winning author or scientific Nobel laureate ever lived at the North Pole or in the Gobi desert. Only when our human needs for warmth, food, clothing, and shelter are satisfied can we turn our attention to creative mental processes.

But what can you do beyond seeing that your child is well fed, dry, clothed, has enough sleep—all the things any caring parent would do anyway? When MacKinnon studied the life histories of creative architects, he found that although all the architects were quite different, their parents behaved similarly when it came to nurturing their children's creativity. Almost without exception, the parents did the following:

1) showed the child an extraordinary respect, almost the same kind of respect they would show to a creative adult;

2) granted their children unusual freedom in exploring their world from a very early age;

3) allowed their children to make their own decisions as much as possible starting very early;

4) gave the child the expectation that the child would act independently but at the same time reasonably and responsibly;

5) avoided developing an intense closeness with the child, the kind that would trigger overdependence, but developed a warm relationship that was liberating and helped the child to feel loved, not rejected;

6) showed a lack of anxious concern when the child wanted to try new things;

7) provided a large extended group of other intelligent adults of both sexes (sometimes, but not always, family members) who could offer other role models for the child;

8) set clear standards on what was right and wrong, but at the same time encouraged the child to develop his own standards of what was right;

9) moved around within a city, or from town to town, or from country to country, which gave the child stimulating new experiences but also helped him to cope with solitude and shyness in strange surroundings;

10) drew the child's attention to the importance of his own thoughts, imagination, and inner mental pictures;

11) allowed their children to develop skills at their own pace, although the development of skills was encouraged;

12) didn't put pressure on their children at an early age to choose a particular profession.

Creative Learning Starts at Home

During the early years of her life, when your child's brain is developing at a faster rate than it ever will again, she learns from everything around her: lamps, keys, food, rugs, pictures on the wall, dogs and cats, the broom, the dishwasher, the telephone.

"When my older daughter was four, we did science in the kitchen," notes Dorothy Rich, who directs the Home and School Institute in Washington, D.C., a national, nonprofit organization whose workshops and publications help parents and teachers help young children learn. While Dorothy Rich was measuring flour, bringing water to a boil, and putting a hard stick of butter into a pan to melt, she was explaining to her daughter in simple terms how science works—about how much flour you need to make a cake, why water gets hot and bubbles, why butter melts over heat and becomes a clear yellow liquid.

What does it mean to start thinking of your own home as a learning center? It doesn't mean you have to run out and spend a lot of money on educational toys and games. It doesn't mean you should start teaching your child to read, write his name, or count to ten. What it does mean is that you'll start looking for natural learning opportunities—like cooking or sorting laundry—and making the most of them by encouraging your child's curiosity. What to you may seem boring or routine, such as vacuuming, is a new game to a toddler.

To an infant, the world of learning is her own crib. As your baby starts to learn about her own abilities—her hands, eyes, feet—she'll start looking, turning her head, reaching and stretching out her arms for objects that interest her. What interests her most is your face, and she'll respond to your smiles and reward you with her own smile beginning at about two months (this is the delightful toothless baby grin called the "social smile").

New York Hospital–Cornell Medical Center psychiatrist Daniel Stern, the researcher who described babies and mothers vocalizing in unison, has found that when mothers and babies gaze at each other, the gazing develops almost a conversational pattern. It's a kind of pre-speech form of communication between parent and infant. The gazing may be accompanied by the mother's talking and the baby's infant cooing or gurgling sounds.

While a dangling mobile will encourage your baby's ability to focus his eyes and his reaching explorations, Burton White cautions against buying mobiles that are pretty objects for parents to look at, but aren't for babies at all. Many mobiles have rather flat objects dangling from them; the objects can be clearly seen by adults who are standing by the crib. But suppose you were lying on your back like your baby? Your plane of vision would be quite different, since you'd be looking up at the object from below. From that position, flat objects would look like the blade of a knife.

An older baby will enjoy active crib stabiles or mobiles that do things by providing rings to pull down. Maybe you don't think of yourself as an educator and your home as a school for creative thought, but when you make the decision to buy a mobile or stabile that really works for your baby and isn't just pretty to look at, that's what you're doing—educating. You're giving your child the chance to start learning from her environment, at her own pace.

Learning Room by Room

When your child is out of her crib and toddling around, the door to home learning opportunities will open even wider. In her workshops, Dorothy Rich likes to help parents think of the home as a school room by room. Start with the kitchen. If you have a set of unbreakable dishes, why not let your youngster help you take the dishes out of the dishwasher and hand them to you, starting with dishes of one size? By watching you put away dishes of the same size in the same place, your child will begin to learn for herself a natural sense of order and classification. A child can stack clean cups or bowls of the same size herself.

When following a recipe, encourage your son to hand you unbreakable items you need, such as a wooden mixing spoon or box of cake mix. Present the cake recipe as an adventure with a beginning and an end product: the cake. "It is very satisfying in any of these activities to come up with a product," notes Rich. The proof of the learning in baking a cake is in seeing and tasting it. In this way you're not *imposing* order or classification on the child, as you would do if you insisted that blocks had to be stacked in a certain way. Rather, the child is learning a sense of order and logical progression of steps, as in making a cake, for himself.

Don't neglect taste when giving your daughter learning experiences in the kitchen. If the child is beginning to talk and wants to know what something is, say the name of the substance and offer her a taste. For example, say the word "cranberry," and explain that cranberry juice tastes sour. Offer the child a tiny taste. Then say "honey" and do the same thing, but explain that honey is sweet. Mix the two together and offer the child a taste, so she can begin to see that substances change their flavor when they are mixed together, as in a cake.

In addition to the kitchen, your family room or living room is also a good place for creative learning. Letting a toddler turn on the light switch gives him his first practical experience of making an electric circuit—though he won't see it quite that way. A bright, active child will simply see that he's made something magical happen by flicking on a switch—all by himself.

Toddlers are fascinated by the telephone, and it is an excellent learning tool. With your help, a young child can dial or punch numbers on a touchtone phone to reach "time" or the weather lady. A young child will delight in punching the buttons himself to reach Grandma in another city. Instead of getting Grandmother's number yourself, let the child do it, first pointing out to him the proper buttons.

A toy telephone or a real phone (unplugged to prevent skyrocketing long-distance bills to Nepal) will keep your toddler happily occupied in creative play. The controlled little hand movements required to dial or press buttons will help your child learn fine-motor coordination as well as find out about how telephones work in people-to-people conversation. A child who is just beginning to talk will have a fine time in pretend conversation.

When you start thinking of your home as a learning center, you'll be surprised at how easily you can turn the most ordinary daily activity into a creative game, to the delight of your child. Sorting, folding, and putting clean laundry into neat piles can become a creative sorting game. It's especially fun for your child to pick out his own T-shirts and overalls among his father's much larger shirts and shorts. You might pile a load of unsorted clean laundry on a bed and let your child go on a treasure hunt for his own clothes in the pile.

Your child can help you fold his clothes after he's found them and even help put them away in his drawers in his own room, again learning naturally how to bring order out of clutter. White athletic socks with different-colored stripes on the top are wonderful learning tools for slightly older children learning to differentiate colors. Letting your child go on a treasure hunt in the laundry pile for the other sock with the red stripe or the other sock with the blue stripe will help him begin to learn color-matching in a creative way, rather than by having you sit him down and say, "O.K., now I'm going to teach you your colors."

All parents, whether they have household help or not, have to do housework. Maybe you think of these household chores as drudgery, but your child doesn't. Young children learn in part by imitating, by trying to do what they see you do. Do you have houseplants? By helping you water them or poke little tabs of plant fertilizer into the soil, your child is learning about what keeps living things healthy and growing. She'll begin to learn that just as she needs to drink her milk to grow, so a plant needs water and fertilizer. Even a toddler can have a seed of her own to water. She can watch a plant sprout from the seed as the weeks pass.

A young child watching you sweep or vacuum will want to do the same. Why not give your child a pint-sized broom (a whisk broom will do) and let him help?

Learning Through Creative Art

It's no accident that art therapy is now being used extensively in mental hospitals to help adults learn to get back in touch with the free-floating creative instincts and happiness they had as young children and lost as they grew older and became more troubled. Through working with materials that respond to a person's inner vision by taking outward shape, both children and adults learn to express their innate personal style and identity. It's important for a highly creative child to feel that she can express her creativity by making something in her home that you will treasure. It might be made of clay, Play-Doh, construction paper, or food coloring (a wonderful "paint" for young children who still occasionally put their fingers in their mouths).

Two is a good age for a child to start exploring art materials on his own, with relatively little direction from adults on "how to make it." Children need adults to provide them with materials and a place to work in harmony, but they don't need or want blueprints. "Too often adults have preconceived ideas about how children's artwork should look," is the view of Martha Browne, an artist/consultant, and June Hopson, a preschool teacher, at the Shady Lane School in Pittsburgh, Pennsylvania. A child's art shouldn't look like anything but what the child wants it to look like. An adult who wants to encourage creativity never asks bluntly, "What

Your Home as a Creative School

is it?" Instead, she or he asks the child in a respectful tone, "Please tell me about your painting [or clay object]."

The problem with coloring books or patterns for objects such as Easter bunnies is that they restrict the creative child's sense of fantasy and fun. Coloring books and cutout patterns are designed by adults according to adult views, and are often trite and unimaginative. A child who stays in the lines or follows the pattern is making a product according to adult direction, not following his own creative instincts.

The philosophy of the Shady Lane School is worth putting into practice at home. In the words of Browne and Hopson: "All creativity grows from playfulness, from the ability to suspend disbelief, from trying new combinations and from risking new ways of doing and thinking. It comes from pretending something that is not. The creative person imagines new possibilities and tests them or sees these possibilities from playing around with materials, activities, or situations. Play presupposes boundaries; but within those boundaries, anything goes."

Your two-year-old can be helped to learn to cut colored construction paper, a complex action that will help him develop eye and hand coordination and get control over the small muscles in his hand. You can put your child on your lap and hold the paper for him until he achieves a sense of mastery with the scissors.

When providing art materials for a two-year-old, remember that the hands are tiny and not yet dexterous (brushes should be short and bristles soft, not firm); clay should be pliable and easily shaped. Remember safety: scissors should be blunt, paints and glue nontoxic. Not giving your child direction about what to make or how to do it does not mean you can't set limits in your home about where artwork is made and where materials go. A two-year-old is not too young to learn that artwork is produced only in the back workroom, or that paint goes on paper, not on him, or his friend, or the walls.

Reward your child for her creative efforts by writing her name on her work (ask her where she wants it to go first, rather than putting it where you want it to go) and by displaying the art. The refrigerator door is a marvelous display space for a child's art, and she can give drawings and clay objects to a parent to take to the office. A visit to the office to see her work displayed there will also help her take pride in what she has created.

Discipline: Home Rule

Turning your home into a creative school does *not* mean turning the house over to unchecked experimentation by small learners getting into everything. While this book does not specifically talk about discipline, helping your child to develop better self-control starts at home and is very much a part of intellectual growth. It's important to view discipline as a learning experience for your child and not a battleground. Fights only waste your and your child's mental resources.

Furthermore, psychiatrists and psychologists have come more and more to look at mental health as the capacity of an individual to reason his way through his problems to a solution, rather than rehashing the mistakes of the past. Obviously none of us, especially a child, can do everything perfectly. But as we grow older we can benefit from what psychologist Albert Ellis calls the "rational-emotive" approach, in which a person is helped to question logically the irrational thoughts which are distorting his emotions and behavior.

In this way, thoughts and feelings aren't considered

mysterious and unknowable, but important parts of ourselves to study and learn about, just as we learn about the functions of our hearts and stomachs. Thus it's important to talk openly about emotions with your child, just as you talk about his toys, the sky and trees, and everything else in his environment. For example, talk to your child about his anger, a powerful force within himself that can either break out irrationally, be dissipated in vigorous physical play such as roughhousing, or later be expressed in words, not actions.

All mental development is based on a child's building of internal control mechanisms which help her put her mind and body to constructive use. The growth of your child's self-regulation and control mechanisms is so important that you as a parent are almost constantly involved in the process.

When a two-month-old is hungry or left alone for long, she cries. She's responding immediately to her basic needs, and she doesn't have too many tools to use to alter her responses. Crying is the most effective tool to get action: it's simple and direct. A two-year-old, on the other hand, doesn't need food instantly; he can be told that lunch is coming soon and that he must wait a minute, or that he can play with his blocks while Mommy talks on the phone.

Development of mastery over our minds and bodies is extremely complicated, but it clearly involves the capacity to delay gratification and rechannel our basic drives. How can you help your child in this process? Since you provide much of the control from the beginning, setting a clear and consistent example in your own behavior at home is very important.

Responding to your baby's cries in approximately the same amount of time every time is much more understandable to her, and therefore more reassuring, than going to her promptly one time, and much later—after she's cried and cried—another. Telling your two-year-old he can't play on the stairs because he might fall and hurt himself should carry the same message every time, and there should be no exception to applying the rule. It shouldn't be O.K. to play on the steps one day and not O.K. the next.

Simply telling your child not to do something—"Don't do that"—often said in an understandably exasperated tone of voice, is the least effective way of helping your child learn and understand self-control. It's an overt power play, with your frustration only reinforcing the impulses in your child which caused him to do "that" in the first place.

There are two basic ways to help your child cope with his emotions and modify his behavior. The first, and in some ways the most preferable, way is to interest your child in alternatives to a behavior which you find absolutely unacceptable. A child will often respond instantly to a new idea, a new initiative, almost as if he's relieved of the stress of a conflict with you, which he doesn't really want. For example, if you find your child playing with an electric lamp cord, you can simply tell him that it's not safe and substitute a long piece of string.

The second approach is to tell your child directly what will happen if he does a certain thing that you don't want him to. This approach makes use of the concept of *contingency*, which a two-year-old is already learning about, and shows him that his actions have real consequences—for good or bad.

Contingencies do stimulate thought, and teach cause and effect in behavior. Very young children are able to understand contingencies ("If I do this then that might happen, while on the other hand if I do this. . .") if they are presented simply and in their frame of reference. You might say, "If you climb on the table you may fall and get a

Your Home as a Creative School

bump," or, "If you climb on the table I will get angry," or, "If you climb on the table I'll spank you."

Remember that any disciplining of your child should be done out of love and respect for him, or it will appear arbitrary, authoritarian, and rejecting. The last thing your child wants is for you to be unhappy with him, and so a compromise solution to behavior problems is usually much easier to find than you might think. Bright, aware children long to please and be loved, and they will rarely act unlovable for long unless unlovable behavior is rewarded.

TV: It's Not Prime Learning Time

In any discussion of creative learning, the subject of television looms in the background. TV isn't really an issue for a baby who is still crawling. A baby may turn her head toward the screen if there's a loud noise, but babies don't really "watch" TV in the sense of being absorbed by it. But toddlers and preschoolers can become absorbed by television. Is TV a fit playmate for your developing child? Or is it simply an inane and sometimes destructive babysitter? Unfortunately, television is for the most part an ineffective or downright harmful babysitter, and the time a child spends watching it is not prime time for learning.

Study after study has revealed the sad truth: too many children watch too much television, and it doesn't do them much good. Alice S. Honig, a professor of child and family studies at Syracuse University who has studied extensively the effect of TV on children, worries about the effect of violent television programs on children from two to seven, who consistently confuse fantasy with reality. Remember that Piaget called this stage in a child's life (which, not surprisingly, is among the most creative) the pre-operational stage, the stage before intellectual reasoning takes over to help the child say, "This is real, and this is not."

Young children "may well believe that what adults on a screen do to hurt each other is the way adults ought to behave or typically act in the real world," Honig has noted. Because a young child watching TV isn't in control, as she is when she creates a piece of art, she can't distinguish fantasy on the screen from real life. Because she can't make that distinction, as she can in her own home, she may try to imitate what she sees as "real." When two children jumped blithely off a roof, trying to imitate Batman flying, they had to be treated for injuries by a doctor (this is a real case).

Research studies have confirmed that young children will imitate the behavior they observe on television. In a 1972 study conducted by Aletha Stein and Lynette Friedrich, ninety-seven preschoolers were divided into groups that watched either "antisocial," "prosocial," or "neutral" TV programs during a four-week period of time. The antisocial programs were twelve half-hour episodes of Batman and Superman cartoons; the prosocial programming consisted of twelve episodes of *Mister Rogers' Neighborhood;* and the so-called neutral programming was composed of children's travelogues. The results of the study indicate that children who watched *Mister Rogers' Neighborhood* were less aggressive, more cooperative, and more willing to share with other children than children who watched the cartoons. Moreover, children who were observed to be slightly aggressive at the beginning of the study became far more aggressive after viewing the Batman and Superman cartoons.

Television is a passive though powerful influence on children, and that goes to the very heart of the learning process. The essence of learning and development is active exploration, not passive acceptance of images on a

Your Home as a Creative School

screen. Your child has to get active feedback on what he's doing: he watches and hears a pile of blocks tumble over after he has piled them too high; he feels the fuzzy back of a kitten to find out what kind of coat it wears; your child wades in waves at the beach to find out what they feel like when they break against his legs.

Learning is also the active two-way process of developing relationships with others, the process psychologists call interaction. "Children struggle through to a more mature understanding of people's motives and feelings as they *interact* with others," notes Honig. "And that is one of the difficult and crucial deficits of TV as teacher. . . . TV watching is a one-way process."

Your child can't ask a robber on a TV show why he's stealing a piece of jewelry from a house; he can't ask a policeman why he shot the robber. He can't taste a new food he sees on TV. He can't touch or shake or poke anything he sees on the screen to find out more about it: the object is on the screen and off again so fast it's gone before your child can even see it properly.

This speedy-image "now you see it, now you don't" style is the very essence of TV as a communications medium: one of the unsettling and anti-learning aspects of video viewing. It's a cheap, quick way to get the attention of a young child, but just getting the child's attention doesn't necessarily mean she'll learn anything. The bright, thoughtful child who desperately wants to reach out and catch a fleeting image, hold it and study it is out of luck.

Most small children simply need more time to digest a concept or explore an idea or object than the few seconds that a TV image may provide. More time: even the very best educational children's shows are plagued by TV's need to be quick about it and get on to other matters because this is costing money.

Research Results Slam TV

Except for a few excellent television programs directed specifically at helping children learn, research studies have almost uniformly condemned TV's influence on young children. In a study done at Harvard University in 1976, children who were found to be "least competent" at solving problems between the ages of two and three watched the most TV. These children were TV junkies. They were allowed to watch fully six hours of TV a day if they chose, and they could watch any kind of program they liked.

In contrast to the young TV junkies, the children who performed the best on problem-solving tests and were considered "most competent" had strict parental guidelines on TV viewing. They could watch for only one hour a day, and it had to be a learning program such as *Sesame Street*.

Research results linking TV viewing to lower achievement "are tricky to interpret," notes Alice Honig. For instance, she cites a 1956 study in which children who watched the most television were inferior in arithmetic and reading skills when they reached school. However, in this study children who were of lower socioeconomic status and tested lower on IQ scales tended to watch the most TV. Therefore, suggests Honig, perhaps the facts of lower socioeconomic status and lower IQ account more for lowered performance and achievement than does the television viewing per se. "There may not be a simple relationship between reading scores and number of television hours logged per week," she notes. A 1964 study suggests that children whose IQ levels test lower than those of other children prefer to watch more television precisely because it is less demanding than active learning. "Teachers and parents need to be alert to the possibility that watching TV is an easier and preferred activity" compared to tasks such as reading that demand more effort, counsels Honig.

Whether or not TV viewing per se causes lower achievement, the simple fact is that children who watch more than one or two hours of TV a day aren't watching children's television; they're watching shows designed for adults with sophisticated tastes, fully developed reasoning powers, a knowledge of what's real and what isn't, and a moral sense of what's right and what's wrong.

If more of television programming time were directly aimed at helping young children learn, television could be an important home learning tool for parents to use, even though it's passive, not active. It could be used to supplement other learning experiences in which your child can touch and explore actively. But a report commissioned by a parents' group called ACT (Action for Children's Television) and done by Boston University communications professor F. Earle Barcus showed that there are very few regularly scheduled TV programs for young children on the commercial networks, especially on weekdays.

As reported by Barcus, fully 29 percent of 588 stations told the Federal Communications Commission (FCC), the governmental agency that monitors television, that they aired no regularly scheduled programs for children between 6:00 A.M. and 6:00 P.M. on weekdays. Even more disturbing was the fact that twice that number—62 percent of the stations—said they had no regularly scheduled programs for children between 2:00 P.M. and 6:00 P.M., the after-lunch and before-dinner time that should be considered prime time for children's learning programs. Special programs on educational television channels simply can't fill the giant gap in children's learning programs left by the commercial networks.

When you realize that more than 98 percent of all American homes have one or more TV sets and that the average child spends twenty-five to thirty hours every week watching television, it becomes clear that our children are viewing adult programs. By the time the typical American child graduates from high school, that teen-ager will have spent about 15,000 hours in front of a TV— a shockingly higher figure than the 11,000 hours he or she will have spent in the classroom—according to figures compiled by ACT.

Captain Kangaroo Dissents

The only regularly scheduled commercial TV program designed especially for young children identified in the Barcus report was "Captain Kangaroo." The lovable character of Captain Kangaroo was created and played by Bob Keeshan. It's worth hearing what Bob Keeshan has to say about television as an influence on children's learning.

"I'm often told I am a parent's best friend, the very best babysitter," Keeshan told members of the National Association for the Education of Young Children. "I am not complimented, although I know the comment to be well meaning. But if all I am is a babysitter, then I do not deserve the investment of a child's time. Time is valuable, even the time of a five-year-old. No! Especially the time of a five-year-old. . . .

"The human being before seven years of age experiences the greatest stage of emotional and intellectual growth, and growth is not a spectator sport." Keeshan went on to note that the television set is unique in American homes because we tend to keep it on even when we're not really paying attention. It's replaced background music from the radio or stereo. In contrast, Keeshan pointed out, we turn off our toaster ovens when the toast is done, and unplug our vacuum cleaners when the rug is clean. It is simply too easy and too much of a cop-out to say to a child, "I'm busy, go watch TV," when TV offers so little.

Many parents believe that Saturday morning is a perfect time for children to watch TV because they can see cartoons. What could be more fun than a cartoon? Unfortunately, the "good fun" of cartoons doesn't make for good viewing for our developing children. Is it good to teach our children to laugh when a cartoon figure falls flat and suffers a squashed nose? Walks off a diving board into a pool with no water? Slams into the side of a house?

Thomas Radecki, an Illinois psychiatrist who chairs the National Coalition on Television Violence (NCTV), testified in Congress that of twenty-five research studies on TV cartoon violence reviewed by NCTV, twenty-four showed "clear trends or proven significant effects that this programming increases aggression and violence in children viewers." And, he might have added, time spent watching these programs decreases the time a child spends in creative learning.

In 1982, the National Institute of Mental Health released a report linking televised violence to aggression, especially in young children and people who are heavy TV viewers. This report essentially said that since a landmark 1972 Surgeon General's report on TV and violence was released, the link between television viewing and aggressive actions has, if anything, grown stronger.

And in addition to the actual programs, remember that children watch commercials between programs. What do young children learn from commercials? For starters: stereotyped images of how women behave (removing rings from shirt collars with laundry detergent) and how men behave (brawling in a bar while drinking beer); that popping a pill will cure almost anything, from arthritis to upset stomach; and that simply using the right toothpaste or deodorant or shampoo will get you the man (or woman) of your dreams.

So, while our children mostly aren't learning creatively from TV, they are learning patterns of violence that could be dangerous to impressionable young minds. It's certainly not what Jean Piaget had in mind when he talked about how important it is for a child to learn moral values.

Creativity is a precious resource that must be treated with respect in order to survive. The extent to which your child can hang on to her most precious gift throughout life will in large part be determined by how you treat that gift when the child is too small to realize that not everyone grows up to be a creative thinker.

Your Home as a School: Natural Learning Opportunities

In the Kitchen:
1. Let your toddler or preschooler taste different substances before you put them in a cake or stew; for example, offer vanilla, sugar, a piece of lemon, bittersweet chocolate.
2. Let a preschooler carefully pour or spoon substances into a measuring cup.
3. If you have a front-loading dishwasher and a set of unbreakable dishes, let your child find the places where the large plates, salad plates, and bowls go and put them in himself.

In the Family Room:
1. Let your child dial the telephone and "talk" to the weather person or to Grandma.

Your Home as a Creative School

    2. Let your child turn a lamp on and off to see what happens to the light bulb.

In the Laundry:
    1. Let your child sort and fold clean clothes.
    2. Help your child to put the clothes in piles, matching them by size.
    3. Encourage your child to match up athletic tube socks by the color bands at the top so he will learn to recognize colors.

NOTE: Limit your child's TV viewing time to an hour or less a day, and select the programs you want him to watch ahead of time so they will be geared for children, not adults. Don't encourage your child to "go watch TV" when he's bored or when you want to pursue an activity without him. Television is a passive, not an active, learning experience.

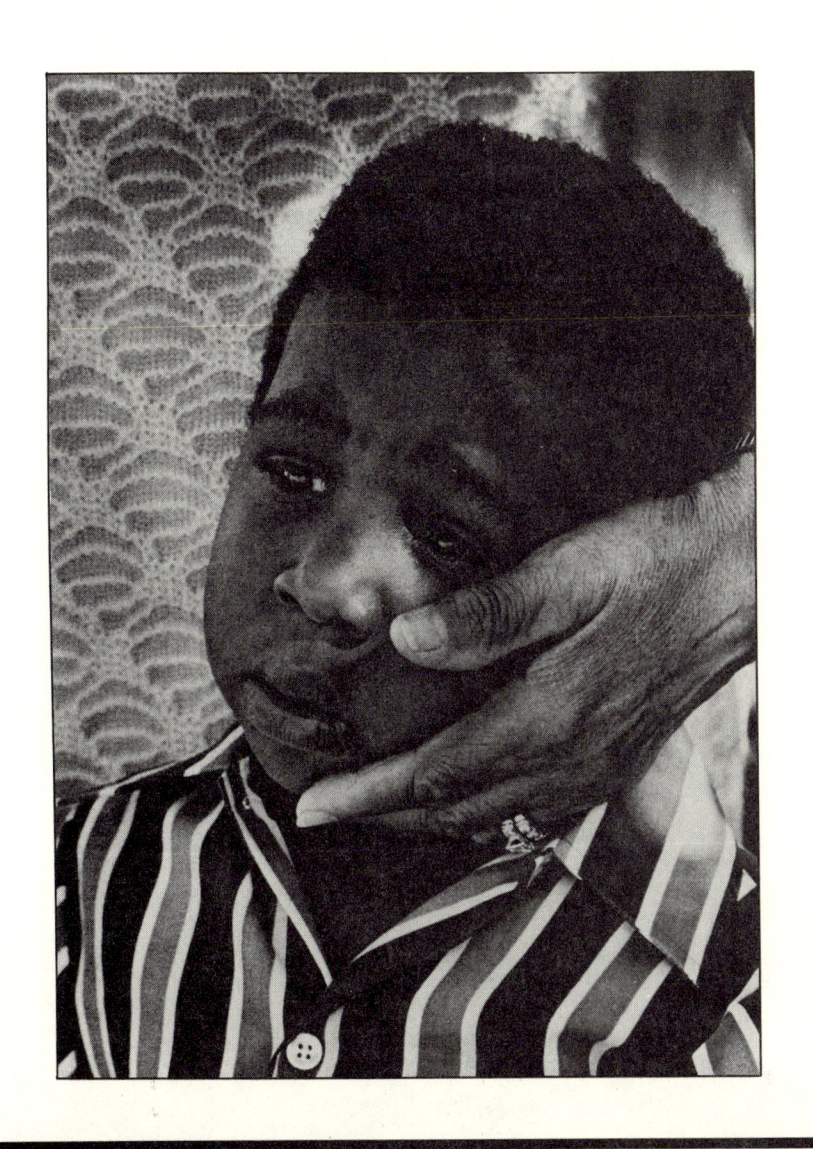

8. Resilience Begins at Home

> For the mind is so dependent upon the humors and the condition of the organs of the body that if it is possible to find some way to make men wiser and more clever than they have been so far, I believe that it is in medicine that it should be sought.
>
> —RENÉ DESCARTES, *Discourse on Method*, 1637

You've probably noticed how efficiently and beautifully your child heals. In a healthy child, a cut closes and the skin smooths out very rapidly, often leaving no scar behind. Wound healing is a good way to measure age; in general, children heal much faster than older people. But there's a lot more to good health than visible healing. Mental health—a quality of resilience and flexibility in the face of stress—is just as important to your child as physical health.

Your baby is a complex combination of mental abilities, moods and emotions, and physical needs. They're all intertwined, so that physical health affects mental and emotional outlook and vice versa. We now know that how a person feels affects the thinking process, and that how a person thinks can affect how he or she feels.

Patterns of thinking and feeling are learned at home, starting in infancy. Harmony between your child's body and mind doesn't just happen; it's learned from parents, cultivated, and practiced. Only recently have scientists begun to understand just how closely the body and mind are linked.

Recognition of that intimate bond has led to exciting new

research that will ultimately help parents to help their children stay well and think more positively and productively throughout their lives. And understanding what scientists know today about how closely the body is linked to the brain can help you to help your child learn to "think himself to health."

The Healing Hand: Background

In the dark days of medicine, the days of bloodletting to release evil spirits, scientists didn't understand how the mind can make us sick or well. They knew there was an intimate connection, but they couldn't pinpoint it. They knew nothing of bacteria and viruses, antibiotics and antiseptics. So they thought physical illness was the result of thinking evil thoughts, or of someone thinking them about you.

If you weren't careful, the evil eye would get you or your family. To ward off evil spirits you put a garlic clove around your baby's neck and carried a lucky charm. Many of us carry rabbits' feet or other lucky charms, a harmless and comforting carry-over from our more superstitious days.

Once, people who were mentally ill were thought to be possessed by demons. If the demons could be exorcised—driven out into the air or into a herd of pigs—then the person could get well again. Drugs to relieve depression or help a person with a severe mental illness like schizophrenia were unknown. Chaining the mentally ill in filthy and brutal asylums was common.

Then the seventeenth-century French philosopher Descartes came along and said "Nonsense" to the evil eye. He literally rescued medicine from a morass of superstition, and helped it grow from a hit-or-miss art into a more exact science.

Descartes saw illness as the product of physical causes, not evil spirits or destructive thinking. Even though he recognized that illness affects the emotions, he made just as clear a scientific division between the mind and the body as if he'd taken a surgical scalpel and cut the two apart.

Today a number of scientists armed with information Descartes didn't have are now going way beyond the seventeenth-century thinker to study the body and mind acting together in health and disease.

These scientists are recognizing that your child's mind can often be as effective a healer as the most powerful drug. They're finding that how we think can literally make us sick. They're also recognizing that positive thinking, starting at an early age, can help us to prevent the harmful effects of stress. And their work is growing more scientific and less speculative as they record what really does happen when the human mind and the human body are happily, healthily in sync. Or totally at odds with each other.

The Mind/Body Connection

In short, scientists now recognize that Descartes was right about separating the mind from the body in disease only up to a point. The result of that realization is a new field of medicine: psychoneuroimmunology. Basically, scientists working in this scientific area try to put together new knowledge from three fields—psychology, brain science, and immunology (the study of the body's immune system, which protects us from disease). They test their theories about how the emotions, the brain, the nervous system, and the immune response all affect one another.

In order to understand why and how new scientific discoveries in psychoneuroimmunology can affect your child, it's important to appreciate what an efficient disease-fighter a healthy child really is. Your child's built-in immune response is a kind of search-and-destroy system geared to ridding the body of foreign substances called antigens that can cause disease. Antigens can be bacteria, viruses, fungi—anything the body recognizes as a harmful invader.

The body has a protective immune system with white blood cells that manufacture antibodies in response to foreign invaders. These protective antibodies build up in response to anything the body interprets as foreign and brands an enemy.

White blood cells perform a variety of essential immunological functions, and without an immune system your child would die. You've probably read about a deadly new disease called acquired immune deficiency syndrome, or AIDS for short. People who develop AIDS have an impaired immune response, possibly due to a virus called HTLV-III recently discovered by National Cancer Institute researcher Robert C. Gallo and his co-workers. This virus appears to attack the white cells that actually direct immune defenses.

The first time your child is exposed to an enemy antigen, she may get very sick. But the next time, owing to the protection of antibodies, your child may be able to ward off disease entirely. What was a major case of the flu (complete with wheezing, coughing, and sore throat) the first time around may be only a little sniffle the next time she encounters the same strain of flu. If the child encounters a new strain of flu, there's very little cross-immunity to protect her, and her body will have to make new antibodies to knock out the new strain.

Maternal antibodies from the mother called gamma globulins cross the placenta and are present in your baby at birth. But they last only about two to three months in your child's circulation. That's why your baby is especially vulnerable to infection when he's under a year old: he hasn't begun to produce his own antibodies in any quantity.

The levels of these disease-fighting antibodies are at a peak in your baby's bloodstream at birth, but they won't be that high again until she is a year old. Nursing during the first year of life can help to protect your baby from disease, because a breast-fed baby keeps right on getting maternal antibodies from breast milk.

Now the question scientists want to answer is whether the mind and the emotions can somehow be trained to help build up this efficient internal disease-fighting system. If parents could learn to coach their children in ways of building up immune defenses—just as they coach them in swimming or math—then they could help them learn how to think their way to health.

It's impossible, of course, to protect your child from all illnesses. But what we have learned from science is that coaching a child to deal with stress is essential to help the child stay healthy. You've probably read about how stress can make us sick. If your child can't learn early to cope with stress, then he will be more susceptible to disease throughout life. The good news is that there are now specific steps parents can take to help their children deal with stress. Before you can help your child cope with stress, it's important to understand exactly what stress is and how it affects your child's body.

The Stress Syndrome

Pioneering Canadian researcher Hans Selye first described the stress syndrome and its effects on disease in the 1930s. In his book *The Stress of Life* (1956), he summarized his important findings from animal studies that show how stress triggers disease.

Selye's most striking finding, while studying rats in a variety of stress-producing situations (chemicals, cold water, tying them down so they couldn't move), was that stress could inhibit the rats' immune systems. Selye found that in stressed rats the tissues that produced the white blood cells and antibodies (the body's infection fighters) actually atrophied, or shrank. So the animals had fewer white blood cells and antibodies protecting them from disease. Regardless of what caused the rats' stress in the first place, if the stress overwhelmed the rats' immune defenses, they would die from disease.

Selye found that stress radically affects our bodies' levels of chemical messengers called hormones. What he found was a large outpouring of the body's natural anti-inflammatory hormones, called corticosteroids—or steroids for short—in the blood of the rats. Inflammation—swelling—occurs when body tissues are injured. The source of the gigantic output of steroids in Selye's rats was the adrenal glands of the animals, which were grossly enlarged.

Steroids are known in medicine to decrease the number of white blood cells and block their function—by preventing them from migrating to sites of infection and producing antibodies, for example. It's clear that the body needs these hormones in naturally occurring levels to suppress an overly strong anti-inflammatory response, which would attack normal as well as diseased tissues.

Doctors use the anti-inflammatory properties of steroids given in high doses as drugs to treat a variety of diseases—leukemia and rheumatoid arthritis, for example. In leukemia, the white cells multiply and grow wildly out of control, while in rheumatoid arthritis the white cells attack normal tissue in joints like the knee and elbow.

However, steroids are a biological double-edged sword, since, as Selye showed us, they weaken the immune system. When your child's body has too high a level of steroids, he is more susceptible to infection because the protective white blood cells don't function as well as they should. Too high a level of steroids can also prevent a cut or surgical wound from healing normally and can even damage the digestive tract enough to cause a bleeding ulcer.

Selye's studies suggested that there are two ways of handling stress, responses that we now believe are learned in childhood. The first way is called "fight or flight." First described by Harvard University physiologist Walter Cannon, this response protects us from immediate physical danger.

The fight-or-flight response prepares the body, by flooding our systems with hormones called catecholamines, to stay and fight an enemy or to flee. They speed up our heartbeat, quicken our reflexes, make us breathe faster, and otherwise put us in a position to face danger. Adrenaline is a major catecholamine hormone. The catecholamine hormones are quite different from the steroids that weaken the immune system. They help us mobilize our energies when we need to be totally alert.

If we learn to control it, the fight-or-flight response can be an ally. It's only when we feel stressed constantly and can't seem to leave that state of "red alert preparedness" that the catecholamines can harm us. In large quantities over time, they can make people more susceptible to heart attack and stroke, among other ailments.

Your child uses the fight-or-flight response all the time, in a natural way. For instance, if his toy is being taken away by another child, he'll grab or hit to get it back (fight). But if the person taking the toy is twice his size, the child may give up the toy for fear of getting hurt (flight). That's normal and healthy.

But the second learned way of dealing with stress isn't very healthy. It's the "loss of control" or "exhaustion" response, and it's marked by passivity and helplessness. People who respond to stress in this way are depressed; they don't believe they can control their lives. And—here's the important point—these people have levels of steroids in their bodies that are often two to three times as high as the normal range.

As we've seen, steroid hormones knock the punch out of the immune system. If depressed people have higher levels of steroid hormones in their systems, it's no wonder they're more susceptible to just about every disease imaginable, including cancer, the most devastating failure of the body's immune system. Numerous studies show that depressed people in general do have more diseases, including cancer.

We now know that children, like adults, can get depressed. If they feel thay have no control over their lives, they'll react with exhaustion and helplessness to stress, not with the healthy fight-or-flight response. In other words, they'll just plain give up.

Now the question scientists want to answer is whether the mind and the emotions can somehow be trained to build up the immune system. Imagine how exciting it would be if you could coach your child on ways of building up the unseen immune defenses. But can the mind really control the immune system beyond helping us react to stress? Up until very recently, scientists thought the immune system operated as a kind of independent guardian angel. Is manipulation of the immune response by our own brains really possible?

The Riddle of the Flavored Water

Robert Ader, a professor of psychiatry and psychology at the University of Rochester School of Medicine and Dentistry and a pioneer in psychoneuroimmunology, thinks this manipulation is theoretically possible. Ader is one of the scientists who now believe that learning mind control over the immune system could happen—someday. In startling laboratory experiments with rats, Ader has proved that learned, coached behavior can actually alter the body's production of antibodies. In other words, immune responses that were previously thought to be completely beyond conscious control and manipulation can be brought under voluntary control—by the mind.

Ader and his co-worker Nicholas Cohen came to their realization about the brain's control over the immune system almost accidentally. They were studying what happens when you give rats water flavored with the artificial sweetener saccharin (which rats normally love) and then add a drug to the water that upsets their stomachs. As expected, the rats immediately started to avoid the saccharin-flavored water because they connected it to getting upset stomachs. This kind of reaction—learned mental conditioning—is exactly what happened in the dogs the Russian researcher Ivan Pavlov trained: the dogs learned to connect food to the ringing of a bell, and when they heard the bell their mouths watered even before they saw the food.

But in addition to the expected Pavlovian response, Ader and Cohen also noticed something else. When the drug that upset the rats' stomachs was removed from the water, the rats went back to drinking more and more saccharin-flavored water. That was expected. But surprisingly, some of these rats died, even though they were young and supposedly healthy and vigorous animals. There was nothing in the flavored water to harm them; the death of these rats was a mystery.

Ader and Cohen took a second look at what they thought originally were fairly simple mental conditioning experiments. They knew that the drug they'd been using that upset the rats' stomachs, cyclophosphamide, also weakens the body's immune system. With a suppressed immune system, rats would be more susceptible to disease, and would die earlier than the normal rat life-span.

But the Rochester scientists were puzzled. They decided that what must have happened is that somehow the rats had been conditioned to suppress their immune response in the absence of the drug. When the rats were being given the drug in the flavored water, their immune response was lowered by the drug as expected. Unexpectedly, however, the rats' brains somehow linked this lowered immune response to drinking the flavored water. So even when the rats were drinking flavored water but weren't being given the drug, they were conditioned to think their immune response was being weakened. And because they believed it, it happened.

Ader and Cohen tested this brand-new "immune-conditioning" theory, setting up different groups of rats and deliberately trying to provoke the immune response in some by giving them sheep red blood cells. A healthy rat immune system will react to the sheep cells as it would to a dangerous foreign invader, and will manufacture antibodies to attack and fight them.

Rats that had learned to suppress their own immune systems—after just one experiment with the drug—didn't produce antibodies to the sheep cells in as high a number as they should have. Their immune defenses were shot down.

Of course, your child is not a rat. It's never smart to say that a response in animals can be applied to humans—without proving exactly that. But to Ader, who has repeated these studies to check his findings, the answer is clear enough: the immune response isn't a totally separate guardian angel, but can be radically changed by the brain. As he himself puts it, "The fact that learning could alter antibody response in this manner demonstrates a clear, direct link between the brain and the immune system."

Recent scientific information has led to a clearer understanding of how the emotions themselves can also play a part in weakening the immune system. Suppose your child is startled by a large dog that growls loudly. Your child mentally processes his reaction in the learning part of the brain, the cortex. The child's reaction to the dog will be partly determined by previous experiences—pleasant or unpleasant. Has he ever been bitten? Did the child approach the dog and try to pat him? Did he try to tough it out and stare the dog down? Did you react to the dog with fear, transmitting your fear to the child?

When a normal, healthy child is afraid, the limbic system of the brain, which is thought to be closely linked to very strong emotions, sends urgent mood signals to the hypothalamus, a sort of master control center of the limbic system. The hypothalamus in turn signals the pituitary gland to start a massive release of hormones like adrenaline—those very catecholamine hormones released in the fight-or-flight response.

There's nothing wrong with conveying a healthy sense of fear to your child. After all, you don't want either of you to be bitten. But if you fall apart and act helpless and powerless before the dog, neither fighting nor fleeing, chances are your child will learn to respond that way too.

He then will have learned to cope with stresses such as the fierce dog with helplessness and the exhaustion response, as if he's at the mercy of the dog and can't control its actions toward him. As we've seen, a feeling of lack of control can cause depression, which triggers a higher-than-normal level of immune-blocking steroid hormones.

Thus the emotions, the brain, and the immune system are all locked in a tight, intimate little circle. Your child will learn to cope with stress with positive behavior that suits the situation—or with helplessness and an exhausted immune system.

The Unsinkable Child

Imagine a person bouncing on a trampoline; resilient children have a mentally bouncy quality when it comes to coping with life's obstacles and problems. They're copers, doers, problem solvers. They don't react with the helplessness that leads to depression. They don't give up.

Scientists are becoming convinced some people develop a helpless, depressed kind of personality way back in childhood that makes them more susceptible to diseases such as cancer—partly because they don't learn to handle stress as well as other people do. Harvard University's George E. Vaillant studied 204 Harvard graduates over a period of forty years to see if, in fact, a positive mental attitude can affect physical health and vice versa.

In a classic report published in *The New England Journal of Medicine* in 1979, Vaillant showed that a healthy mental outlook can help keep people from getting sick in middle age. In contrast, people who have a defeatist or unhealthy outlook on life tend to become physically sick.

In Vaillant's study, the men who became sick in middle age tended to be depressed (which, as we have seen, weakens the immune system), anxious, and emotionally troubled. Vaillant concluded that "stress does not kill us so much as ingenious adaptation to stress (call it good mental health or mature coping mechanisms) facilitates our survival."

When Vaillant reached back to look at these men's childhoods, he found that the unhealthy men who didn't have a positive mental outlook had relationships with their parents when they were children that didn't lead to feelings of control. As children, the men didn't learn from their parents a sense of initiative, independence, or trust.

People who don't learn a sense of control in childhood grow up to be disease-prone adults. They tend to be passive, nonassertive individuals who have trouble expressing their emotions and forming close relationships with others. The men Vaillant studied who fell into this group had many more job problems and failed marriages than the men in other groups.

Such people aren't very resilient; they don't seem to have developed coping methods as children that help them deal effectively with problems. They don't bounce back. They haven't developed a necessary sense of competence, a sense that what they think and do matters in controlling what happens to them.

Joan Borysenko, a cell biologist and psychologist who teaches at Harvard Medical School, is one of a number of scientists who are probing how the emotions affect the immune system to make a disease such as cancer more or less severe.

"A feeling of control seems to be very important" when it comes to fighting cancer, in Borysenko's words. "As a group, the people who feel they are fighting back, who seek to gain some kind of control over events, survive longer than the more passive group. If stress is the difference between the perceived threat and the perceived ability to cope, and stress depresses the immune system, then we would expect the non-copers to have poorer outcomes. And they do, according to the available studies." In other words, people who as children didn't learn how to cope with stress are candidates for a weakened immune response—and thus disease—when they grow older.

Borysenko and many other scientists in the new field of psychoneuroimmunology believe that there are cancer patients whose bodies manage to exist "in dynamic equilibrium" with disease while their immune defenses are working. But then a stressful event happens that essentially weakens the immune response. Maybe it's the loss of a close relative or a job; maybe it's a move to a new city where everybody seems strange and unfriendly. This stressful event, which puts a damper on the body's own defenses, shifts the balance in favor of the disease, and cancer ultimately wins.

We are still a long way from being able to teach children how to manipulate their own immune systems to stay well. Yet the growing body of evidence on how closely the mind and body are linked is yielding new and fascinating information about staying healthy, information parents can use.

For example, although researchers used to think of depression as a strictly adult illness, they now know that children, too, are capable of succumbing to this serious mood disorder. For this reason it's important to help your child learn to cope with feelings of sadness. Encourage your child to talk about her feelings so she can learn that emotional ups and downs are normal and natural, and that you do not expect her always to be or act happy. Explain to her that everyone—adults and children—feels sad occasionally, and that there's nothing wrong with the feeling. Let her know that her sadness is only temporary and that she will not always feel sad.

When you think your child may be having a difficult day emotionally, plan something special for the two of you, such as a walk in nearby woods where you can both look at the wild flowers and trees in tranquillity. By planning special mood-lifting trips for you and your child beyond the home environment, you're helping him learn how to lift himself out of the emotional doldrums. If you simply let your child indulge in feeling glum (which is different from openly expressing his feelings of sadness) you'll miss a chance to show him that he has some control over his feelings, and that there are alternatives to moping. Israeli psychologist Shlomo Breznitz has pointed out that children are natural hopers who have great resilience of spirit. In his studies of the psychology of hope, he has concluded that many Western parents underestimate their children's ability to cope with feelings of sadness and distressing events, such as the death of a pet or a terrifying nightmare.

If you overreact with concern and nervousness to the death of the pet or to the nightmare, your child—who may be naturally resilient in spirit—might begin to do the same. Allow your child to grieve for the pet and accept the fact of death. While it's perfectly all right to comfort a child who has had a nightmare by taking him into bed with you, you might want to consider putting a dim night-light in the child's room to show him that the night does not hold terrors he cannot see. When you come into his room to comfort him, he will be able to see your face, which will further help him orient himself to his waking state and forget shadowy terrors of the mind. In this way you'll be helping your child develop his own healthy patterns of reacting to disheartening or fearful events.

Perhaps the most important message from all the studies on psychoneuroimmunology is that mental and physical health aren't preordained. Of course inheritance has a lot to do with whether your child will be susceptible to certain physical or mental illnesses that run in families, but that's only part of the story.

In the next chapter we'll look at specific ways of applying what scientists now know about the body/mind connection to help our children stay well. We'll learn how to help children shun learned helplessness, passivity, and panic. We'll learn how a sense of competence can be cultivated—by caring parents.

There is no question that resilience begins at home.

9. Making Control Count

> Nothing paralyzes your efficiency more than frustration; nothing helps it more than success.
>
> —HANS SELYE, *Stress Without Distress*

What a young child finds out very early about controlling his environment is crucial for his development. If his cries bring milk and a loving parent's face, then he will begin the long process of developing a sense of self and mastery of his world. If he cries when he's hungry and wet and nothing happens, the child will learn to be helpless. He will become listless and depressed.

Babies in orphanages who learned this helplessness role were often called "failure-to-thrive" babies. As we've seen, they tended to become sick because depression weakened their immune systems.

As is true for all of us, when a child masters an easy task it makes the next task easier. If you give your child a toy which is beyond his ability to use because his hands haven't developed fine enough coordination, the toy will teach only frustration and failure as the child tries again and again to do what—physically—he's not ready to do. Such toys only produce stress. But if you give him toys or games that build on each other, growing more difficult in logical order, the child will develop a sense of worth, mastery, and confidence.

Control and Kiddie QR

As infants grow and develop into children, it's important for them to learn control as well as a sense of mastery. In the last chapter, we looked at the quality of resilience, that buoyancy that allows children to cope with stress healthfully. Resilient children learn a sense of control that's flexible, not rigid. The kind of control that works for your child will allow for individual achievement. It won't be an intellectual or emotional straitjacket. Your child will learn about gaining control from you, from other children, and later from teachers.

Building on the work of Hans Selye, a number of scientists have studied ways of relaxation that can help both children and adults to cope with stress and gain a sense of control over events. Stress becomes distress when we feel out of control. Using techniques of relaxation to relieve stress has a long and honorable history; throughout the centuries Eastern thinkers have extolled the virtues of learning to relax. Yoga and meditation are Eastern gifts to stressed Western men and women.

Recently, researchers have found that children as well as adults who learn the life-giving art of relaxed control have an edge when it comes to coping with stress. Charles F. Stroebel, a Connecticut physician in private practice and former research director of the Institute of Living, in Hartford, has developed a relaxation technique called the quieting reflex (QR for short) that helps people cope with stress.

Stroebel's co-worker, Margaret Holland, has successfully adapted the six-second technique for young children. It's called kiddie QR. The whole rationale behind the quieting reflex is that during the fight-or-flight response (that state of physical readiness we looked at in the last chapter), when our bodies are flooded with red-alert hormones such as adrenaline, we react in a predictable way with five major physical results, or stress symptoms.

1. We pay increased attention to whatever's causing our stress, with heightened senses of sight, hearing, and smell.

2. We perspire, our hands feel wet, and a blush spreads up over our faces.

3. The muscles in our faces become tense and we breathe in shallow gasps.

4. Our hands and feet feel cold and clammy, and their temperature actually drops.

5. Our jaws are clenched grimly, as if we're gritting our teeth.

Like the adult version of QR, kiddie QR is designed to reverse all these five steps—in a six-second response that becomes second nature when you've done it enough.

A teacher or a parent instructing in the QR technique teaches a child to recognize the physical factors outlined above. Getting the child to recognize he's under stress is the first step in getting him to know how to cope with it. Here's how the reversal would work if a child were trying it:

1. The child becomes aware of exactly what is causing the stress. He wants something he can't have, for example.

2. Instead of a frown or cry, you teach your child a "sparkle smile," which helps to relax tense facial muscles and a tense jaw.

3. You have the child take an easy deep breath and let his jaw go limp. Then he breathes out, exhaling slowly, and you suggest that there is a "wave of warmth and heaviness" going down to his toes. (You can't be tense while doing this exercise—try it.)

Kiddie QR is basically learned self-regulation. Stroebel and Holland feel it should be taught with supervision, and say that it shouldn't be taught to children with certain medical conditions, such as diabetes or seizures. (If it works, the child's lowered state of arousal—which is the whole point of QR—could precipitate a seizure or mask an insulin reaction.)

Kiddie QR probably isn't for toddlers who can't talk yet, because it would be too difficult to get across its concepts. But even a very young child who observes a parent applying the QR technique can begin to get the idea of how it works. A toddler, who is smart enough to pick up cues from a parent and imitate them, can watch you and pick up the QR cues from what you do. Why not try using QR the next time you feel stressed—when a clerk refuses to take back a purchase at a store, for example?

Kiddie QR is simply a way of helping children pause, take a quick breather, and learn to control their own actions. The pause gives them time to respond to a situation with thought—not with tears or a tantrum. And kiddie QR has been used in a number of school systems to help children who disrupt classrooms with boisterous behavior. Some parents and teachers informally use quieting methods—a moment of silence, for example—without having studied the techniques of QR, in order to calm excited children.

"We find that the great majority of young people, as they become proficient in evoking the Quieting Reflex, gain a new sense of freedom," in the words of Margaret Holland. "They recognize that many of the problems which have disturbed them in the past are not beyond their voluntary control."

Adds Holland, "Their new sense of mastery with QR leads to enhanced self-concept and an ability to use their full potential in ways that their parents, they and their teachers previously had thought impossible."

Kiddie QR isn't a magic formula that can automatically confer good mental and physical health on your child. It's simply one proven technique designed to help the child gain control and a sense of self-esteem. The technique is only as good as the child's use of it. But without the self-mastery and control a technique like kiddie QR helps to foster, your child is inviting stress-related problems that may catch up with him later.

Straight Thinking

In addition to helping us understand what happens in children's bodies when they're under stress, research on what leads to resilience has yielded some fascinating information about the way they think. Psychologists are finding that the "power of positive thinking" doesn't just happen—it can be learned at an early age, cultivated, and practiced.

George Spivack and Myrna B. Shure, both professors of mental health sciences at Hahnemann University in Philadelphia, have identified a system of "straight thinking" that helps children resolve problems that used to frustrate them and put them under stress. It's called interpersonal cognitive problem-solving, which has been shortened simply to ICPS.

ICPS research studies, which are funded by the National Institute of Mental Health (NIMH), are now being conducted around the country. The skills, which are being used to help physically abused children and those who are disturbed by their parents' divorces, have been taught in Philadelphia-area and Michigan preschools. ICPS is now being taught to older children in Philadelphia public grade schools as well.

As described by researchers Spivack and Shure, the ICPS way of thinking involves five special skills that can be learned and practiced by young children:

1. The ability to think of alternative solutions to problems, called "optional thinking."

2. An aptitude for "means–end" thinking, a planned strategy of determining what you want to get and how best to get it.

3. The ability to consider the consequences of your actions, in terms of their impact on others and on yourself.

4. The sensitivity to perceive that how you feel and act may have been influenced by (and may have influenced) how others feel and act.

5. A special sensitivity—a kind of emotional radar—to the potential existence of problems whenever people get together.

These five skills aren't personality traits, nor are they mere expressions of your child's level of intelligence as measured on a standard IQ test. They are thinking skills we all develop naturally to a greater or lesser degree. Children who develop ICPS skills to a greater degree while young tend to be resilient and to have a more positive view of their own abilities. "Studies have shown that when people learn these skills, generally their self-esteem goes up," in Spivack's words.

The Philadelphia researchers have tested ICPS skills with impulsive preschoolers, children whose actions can spell trouble later when they enter first grade. Impulsive children aren't likely to stop to think of alternative solutions to problems. Instead, they may scream and stamp their feet to get their way. They are frustrated easily and often use physical force to make other children obey them. They don't consider how other children feel.

When trained in ICPS skills, impulsive four- and five-year-olds learn to wait for a turn, stop nagging and demanding, and stop using physical force to get their way. "We believe that even very young children can, or can learn to, think for themselves and solve everyday interpersonal problems," write Shure and Spivack. "Those who can do this are likely to be better adjusted than those who cannot."

The ICPS nursery program for young children uses a clear, simple script that introduces the children to words important in basic problem-solving in twenty-minute lessons over a three-month period. The lessons aren't presented as lessons at all—they're presented as games.

The children learn the concepts behind the word "not" so they can later decide what to do and whether something they've thought of doing is really a good idea. They learn the word "or" so they can think of alternative solutions to common problems, as in "I can do this or I can do that." They also learn the concept behind the word "different," which helps them to think of different (alternative) things to do.

After about eight weeks, the children are shown pictures and puppets that highlight the important ideas behind the words they have learned to use. For example, using the puppets a child might improvise a scene in which he tries to get a visiting child to help him pick up his toys. There are a number of ways he could approach the child.

He could threaten the visitor ("I'll hit you if you don't help me"), bribe and reward ("If you help me I'll let you play with my puppy"), or ask the child straight out to help him in a social way ("Will you help me pick up my toys?").

The parent or teacher who is getting across ICPS skills with the puppets could use them to help the child see what kind of response each of his actions would provoke. Let us say that one puppet is taking the part of the child who wants help with his toys and the other puppet is taking the part of the visitor.

Threatened with hitting, for instance, the puppet might hit back. Asked to accept a bribe, the puppet could react in such a way that the child realizes fully that what he's done is to try to buy cooperation. For example, the puppet might say, "I want to do more than play with your puppy if I help you. I want you to give me your green racing car." The child would most likely be outraged and withdraw the original offer of a bribe/reward.

The parent or teacher who is helping to get across ICPS skills to a child doesn't make judgments about a course of action or say something's a bad idea. Rather, he helps the child draw conclusions for herself. This point is important, because the aim of ICPS is to help the child learn to think for himself, not follow orders.

Imagine that a mother has entered the room to find her son, Ben, aged four, loudly screaming and grabbing for his wooden horse, while a visiting playmate, Joey, is stubbornly clutching the horse. The mother could order Ben to stop grabbing for his toy, and angrily tell her child that when friends come to visit he should share his toys. She could also threaten not to let Ben play with Joey again if they can't learn to play "nicely" together.

But the mother who's using ICPS skills doesn't order or threaten. Instead, she might ask Ben, "What happened? What's the matter?" Depending on what Ben says, she might say (without taking sides), "You're mad and your friend Joey is mad. Can you think of a way of getting your horse back from Joey so you both won't be mad?"

This statement will help Ben stop and realize that he and Joey are getting nowhere, and that maybe he ought to try another tactic. His mother's words might suggest to Ben that he try some other method with Joey, such as the idea of taking turns. Then Ben, not his mother, might himself come to the point where he could say on his own, "You can play with my horse a little longer, then I want him back."

A teacher who is using the ICPS methods doesn't order a child to do something; she helps him think of it for himself. For instance, in a situation described by Shure and Spivack, a child asked his teacher for some Play-Doh. She told him she couldn't get it for him right away because she was helping a child who was hurt. She then asked the child if he could think of something else to do until she had finished helping the hurt child. The child who wanted the Play-Doh thought for a while, and then said, "I'll go paint." If the teacher had merely ordered the child to go paint in the beginning, the child might have said, "I don't want to paint, I want the Play-Doh."

In these studies with ICPS skills, the ability of four- and five-year-old children to think of alternative solutions to common problems in their everyday lives surfaced as the strongest influence on the children's behavior. The ability to see and think beyond one goal, and one way to get it, seems to be the key in the ICPS story. "They must learn to cope with frustration when they cannot have their wish," as the Philadelphia researchers put it.

Why does ICPS work? Why does the National Institute of Mental Health regard gaining these straight-thinking skills as important for everyone who wants to stay mentally healthy? "We believe it has to do with the ability to think for oneself," comment Spivack and Shure.

"Instead of teaching adult-valued 'good' ways to solve

problems, young children were taught to consider alternatives and the consequences. The goal was not immediate resolution of the problem. It was more important to help the child recognize the problem, what might have led up to it, and to consider the various solutions available." ICPS allows children to develop a sense of control themselves. Control is not something imposed on them; it comes from within.

Learned Helplessness

When you teach your child simple coping techniques like kiddie QR or ICPS, you're helping him become independent and develop a sense of competence and control over events and situations. There is increasing scientific evidence that parents who help their children to develop this independence of thought and inner sense of control help them to stay physically and mentally healthy as they grow older. In contrast, parents who don't allow their children to learn to think independently can make them more susceptible to stress.

These parents may think they're doing their child a favor by creating a cushy world where she gets everything done for her without effort. They'd probably be shocked if you told them they can unintentionally help to make their children become ill later in life when stresses overwhelm them.

As we've seen, the immune system's sensitivity to stress is one of the newest and most exciting research findings about the body/mind connection. But there are other important psychological reasons why children who fail to develop independence of thought and a sense of self-esteem break down under stress.

Children have an uncanny ability to act according to your

expectations. Educators know the "expectation principle" and now try to avoid branding a child with any kind of derogatory label, such as "slow learner." A child who is branded a slow learner may say, "Why should I try hard? Nobody thinks I can learn as fast as other kids, so I won't."

If you expect your child to try to solve problems independently, chances are he will try to do exactly that. If you expect your child to learn control and forgo tears and tantrums, he'll probably develop that sense of inner control. If, on the other hand, you do most things for him, he will grow to expect this from other people throughout his life.

At its extreme, doing everything for a child can lead to the child's assuming what psychologists call "learned helplessness" or a "sick role." In the beginning, when a child is a tiny infant, doing for him is vital. He must learn that he can count on you to feed him when he is hungry or change his diaper when he is wet. That's a sign to him that he's mastering and controlling his environment. But you can meet his physical needs while helping him to master the world for himself.

The child who has received the learned helplessness or the sick role message from his parents is a smart child. He is smart enough to exploit the message he's getting. Why should I bother doing it for myself when Mom will do it? he asks himself. If he has been pampered while sick, he is smart enough to perceive that sickliness gets him lots of attention. He may fall into the sick role precisely because he likes the pampering and he sees that playing sick is a good way of getting attention and keeping it.

Being sick may get you special meals in bed. Being sick may get you presents. And certainly if you're sick you don't have to pick up your toys or dress yourself.

Consider the case of four-year-old Kevin. Kevin had

several long and serious bouts of illness as a toddler. He learned that when he was sick he could throw tantrums and not get scolded. He learned his mother would bring him special treats to eat.

Kevin, being a bright child, learned to read the expression on his mother's face as deep concern and worry, and he liked the attention. So he started doing something else to get a little extra attention. Although toilet-trained, Kevin started purposely messing in his pants when he was sick. He learned that his mother wouldn't scold him for not going to the potty then. Kevin began to use his bowel movements as a way of getting attention. Later, when he was a little older, Kevin learned to mess in his pants and feign sickness. It always brought his mother running with that look of concern on her face.

The trouble with learned helplessness is that the child like Kevin who falls into these patterns will be ill-equipped to deal with a world that treats him with greater indifference. Learned helplessness isn't effective in school or on the job.

Worse, a smart child like Kevin may actually do such a good job at playing sick and helpless that he actually convinces himself that he is ineffectual and sickly.

The Phobic Trap

Parents of little girls have to be especially careful not to instill a sense of learned helplessness in their children. A girl looks like a fragile and dainty creature who needs protection, an exquisite doll who must be pampered. But new psychological research on women who have phobias—strong, irrational, and often disabling fears—shows that some were overprotected when they were children.

Making Control Count

You may have read about women who have agoraphobia, a crippling fear of leaving the home. Women who have severe agoraphobia (from the Greek, meaning "fear of the marketplace") literally believe they will die or go mad if they open their front doors and leave their houses. The danger isn't real, but that doesn't mean anything to the phobic; to her the fear is real and absolutely terrifying. Agoraphobia is the phobia that most often sends people to phobia clinics for help; most of the patients who have agoraphobia are women, and this mental disorder is often called "the housewife's disease."

Barry Wolfe, a National Institute of Mental Health researcher, is one of a number of scientists who now believe that an overprotected traditional feminine upbringing can help to make a little girl agoraphobic later. Women who were raised to feel dependent on someone else, who were not encouraged to think for themselves, are more likely to fear the outside world, retreat to the safety of the home, and stay there, he believes.

Not all scientists believe upbringing influences the development of phobias. The cultural and behavioral explanation for phobias does not hold up for all women who have agoraphobia, and it is certainly not the whole story. Doctors now know that agoraphobia can be triggered in some women by a biochemical condition that causes panic disorder, attacks of disabling fear that seem to come out of the blue. Because they now know that biochemically induced panic attacks can lead to agoraphobia, some doctors are using drugs to try to block the panic attacks. These medications include tricyclic antidepressants and monoamine oxidase (MAO) inhibitors, two classes of drugs used to treat depressed patients. But as is often true in psychiatry, biochemistry and cultural conditioning may both be contributing factors in some cases of phobic women; biochemistry does not necessarily preclude the effects of cultural conditioning, or vice versa.

A sense of sexual identity is instilled in a girl at a very young age. By the time she turns three, a little girl has a realization that she is indeed a girl. This sense of being a girl (which is very important to her identity) is reinforced by her hair and clothes, which tell her she is different from boys.

But if the little girl receives other messages along with the hairstyle and the clothes, she can begin to develop the early fears that can lead to phobias later, according to Wolfe. Those messages likely to be transmitted are the traditional ideals we all think of as feminine: softness, delicacy, gentleness, dependence, passivity, and submissiveness.

Girls raised to be dependent develop what Wolfe calls a "crippled potential for mastery" and "an enduring hope of protection." Raised this way, he notes, a little girl doesn't have much of a chance of being mentally healthy. "With such a self-concept, it is easy to see why a woman may become extremely anxious when faced with difficult decisions, complex tasks, and the possibility of loss of primary loved ones."

By encouraging your child—girl or boy—to develop independence of thought, a strong sense of self-esteem, and control that comes from within, you're helping to avoid the possibility that the child will fall into helpless, dependent, or fearful roles that could lead to mental and physical problems later. As a parent you have choices in the way you handle events at home, choices that will affect what your child does throughout life.

Pain Without Panic

Suppose, for example, that you react with fear and panic when you cut your hand or when your child cuts a hand. Your child could develop a low tolerance for pain. While everybody's pain threshold—the level at which they feel something hurts—is about the same, people have very different tolerances for pain. The pain threshold has been defined as "the least stimulus intensity at which a subject perceives pain." Pain tolerance, on the other hand, has been defined as "the greatest stimulus intensity causing pain that a subject is prepared to tolerate."

In some very stoical societies, people can feel pain, but tolerate it. People in these societies learn while still young to tolerate pain, not go to pieces when they feel it. Where do children learn how to experience and tolerate pain? From their parents. If you react calmly to a scrape or bump and help your child to do the same, you're giving the child confidence that everything is going to be fine. The child picks up cues on how to react from you.

Chances are that a child who sees that a parent can't control a reaction to pain won't develop a sense of control himself. Later, as an adult, he'll overreact to a minor bump or scrape. He may fear going to the dentist, face a surgical operation with terror. Being able to face pain with a certain amount of stoicism, on the other hand, will benefit your child when he's in a situation where pain tolerance is needed.

If you tend to panic in medical emergencies, maybe you need to examine your own childhood to see if you were raised to overreact to pain, injuries, and blood. If you know you tend to panic in medical emergencies, try consciously to control that reaction and express outward calmness. Of course, some injuries appear so severe you'll want to get to the hospital immediately. But it pays to be calm and reassuring when taking stock of the situation. The cut may need a Band-aid and a kiss, not stitches. And your child will learn in turn that a minor cut is not a cause of panic.

The Power of the Placebo Effect

The signals you send your child can go a long way toward building health and stamina and a sense of control from an early age. That's partly due to something called the placebo effect. This is a truly miraculous emotional effect that parents, as well as doctors, use to their children's advantage every time they convey a sense of wellness and competence.

The word placebo is the Latin word meaning "I shall please." Doctors use the word to mean an inactive substance, such as a sugar pill, given to make a patient feel better. The word placebo has been broadened to mean any kind of nonspecific treatment—mental or physical—designed to help someone feel better.

When you put a Band-Aid on your child's scraped knee and finish it off with a hug, you're using the powerful placebo effect. It's not the Band-Aid that does the trick. It's your positive attitude. You instill a sense of wellness and control in your child, and she immediately feels better.

In scientific studies, the placebo effect as used by doctors has lessened pain, stemmed nausea, and relieved a variety of ills including ulcers, menstrual discomfort, hay fever, and depression. What the placebo effect shows is the strong power of suggestion as a healing force.

Scientists now believe that there may be a remarkable natural phenomenon behind that power of suggestion: the release of powerful pain-killing substances in the brain called endorphins. Endorphins are a little like the drug morphine—strong (but natural) substances that have the same effect as opiate drugs.

Studies by Charles W. Denko at Fairview General Hospital in Cleveland have shown that people with arthritis, who are in chronic pain, have lower levels of endorphins in their blood than healthy people. Can the placebo effect actually trigger the release of endorphins in the brain? Can the power of suggestion deliver a biochemical as well as an emotional uplift? If further studies prove that it can, then helping your child feel better may really be as simple as convincing the child he or she actually *is* better.

It's possible now to help your child learn ways of thinking that will help him cope with stress. Learning to deal with stress and frustration can help him to remain well. When your child is having trouble doing something you know he can do, such as fit a puzzle piece into one of his more difficult puzzles, don't simply take the piece and put it into the indentation yourself. Putting the piece in yourself, especially when you know your child can do it, is nonproductive because it does nothing to foster the child's sense of competence and self-esteem. Suggest that he try to put the piece in another way—turn it around, for example. Or divert the child's attention to another puzzle piece—or even try another toy—to help him "unplug" from the frustrating situation, without resolving it for him. When he returns to the piece that stumped him, he'll have a fresher outlook.

When your child wants to do something you won't allow, try not to fall back on that old standby answer for why it's not permitted: "Because I say so." Following direct orders without explanation doesn't help a child develop an inner sense of control. A bright, curious, but obedient child who wants to please may follow the order but have many unanswered questions that need answering to foster a sense of inner control. Why don't you approve of what she wants to do? If your child's friends are doing it, why can't she? A bright, curious, but very independent child may try to do whatever you've forbidden anyway, thus risking punishment. In the case of the first type of child, you're imposing your own sense of control, not helping the child find her own. In the case of the second type of child, you're encouraging disobedience by not offering a rational explanation for your decree.

Similarly, threats when your child is misbehaving, like decrees when he wants to do something you won't permit, also do not help him develop a sense of inner control and the ability to handle stress. For example, if your child and a friend are fighting over one of your child's favorite toys, don't threaten the child to play nicely or you won't let any of his friends come over to visit. Sharing as a concept means nothing to a young child. Therefore, making threats about not letting friends come back to play if he won't share his toys will be wasted effort. Try to help your child step back and realize that he and his friend are getting nowhere. Try saying something like "Both of you want to play with the same toy. Can you think of a way each of you can get to play with the truck so you'll both be happy instead of mad at each other?" Helping the child to think of alternative behavior himself will help him to develop a sense of control that's flexible enough to allow for other solutions, but not so passive and nonconfrontational that he turns into a doormat for others when faced with a situation of conflict.

Your child is smart enough to try to manipulate any situation to suit himself. But manipulation of situations is no substitute for the kind of learned control that counts. How you help your child develop that kind of learned control—

inner control—will go a long way toward helping him cope with stress and accomplish what he wants to do.

The holistic health movement, which focuses on the total person, not just one organ or disease, has gone a long way toward helping us recognize that physical and mental health is far more within our own control than we thought. For example, scientists now know that it is possible to train adults to lower their blood pressure through biofeedback, hooking them up to a machine that lets them look at and learn to control their blood pressure readings. Adults can also learn to lower blood pressure simply through relaxation techniques.

As we learn more about promoting health at earlier ages, it may soon be possible to develop a blueprint for training children to strengthen their natural defenses against disease. Meanwhile, through the use of techniques such as kiddie QR and ICPS and the powerful placebo effect, we can help our children to react and think independently, and to develop the self-control necessary to cope with stress—and their own wants and needs—effectively.

10. Beyond Bonding: Fathers Are Parents, Too

> To the evident surprise of many investigators, all studies have shown that fathers can be quite as competent and responsive as mothers and that young infants clearly develop attachments to both parents, although most babies preferentially seek comfort from their mothers when they are in distress.
>
> —MICHAEL E. LAMB, *American Psychologist*

Shortly before he was killed outside his New York apartment in 1980, ex-Beatle John Lennon told radio interviewers that his life revolved around his five-year-old son Sean. In the final years of his life, it was fatherhood that brought Lennon his greatest joy; in one of the last intimate pictures taken of him, a photographer caught the musician looking down tenderly at little Sean during a pause while shaving in the bathroom.

A small group of psychologists who have studied fathering showed little surprise that a famous musician should publicly declare his sense of fulfillment in being a househusband and father. Fatherhood and the concept of fathers as stimulating, loving caretakers for their children are finally beginning to achieve recognition among researchers.

Up until the early 1970s, most research on parents and children was really research on mothers and children. "Not long ago, men in our culture neither sought nor assumed active responsibility for the rearing of their children," points out Michael E. Lamb, professor of psychology, psychiatry, and pediatrics at the University of Utah and a pioneering researcher in the field of fathering. Lloyd de

Mause's comprehensive book *The History of Childhood* gives fathers short shrift and little space. The warmest gesture of an American father to his child during the eighteenth century seems to have been a formal letter expressing mild interest in the child's activities or a present after a long absence.

Bonding with the Father

Publicity about bonding as a magical moment that takes place between mother and child shortly after birth has had some good and some not-so-good fallout for parents. Bonding has been portrayed largely as a woman's experience: the newborn is placed on his mother's stomach and a magical emotional glue is secreted from somewhere that ties the two together forevermore. It's a limited and scientifically inaccurate portrayal that can leave mothers feeling inadequate and disappointed if they don't experience some overwhelming rush of warmth for the new little being. In the view of Phyllis W. Berman, a researcher with the Human Learning and Behavior Branch of the National Institute of Child Health and Human Development, it also cuts out adoptive mothers. Worse, where does this fairy-tale version leave Dad?

There is no evidence that a father can't be as good a parent-teacher for a bright, active child as a mother. While it is true that female hormones play a major role in pregnancy and birth, the ability to parent effectively isn't determined by hormones, but by loving concern. There is no such thing as a "mothering hormone." Other than breastfeeding, fathers can do just about anything for their babies mothers can do. Neglect of fathers' role as an important influence on their children—especially during infancy—stems from the fact that traditionally mothers have per-

Beyond Bonding: Fathers Are Parents, Too

formed most of the caregiving activities for babies.

Certainly mothers have always been more deeply involved in raising children than fathers, especially if you consider that prenatal care—the nine months or so a woman nurtures a developing fetus in her body—is the woman's responsibility. And in traditional societies, mothers have always stayed home to raise children while fathers went out to grow or build or labor to pay for their families' food and shelter. Since this was true, it was assumed that mothers were somehow better at parenting than fathers; and since they spent the most time with their children, it was assumed they must be the most important developmental influences on their children. The phrase "maternal and child health" has become part of our working vocabulary, used by doctors, psychologists, and policy-makers in Congress who allocate money to research. There is no comparable phrase for fathers: "paternal and child health."

Fortunately for fathers who actively seek a major role in helping their babies develop and learn, babies themselves don't happen to agree with the common assumption that mothering has to be done mostly or only by mothers.

The New Fathers

Times are changing and so are fathers. Only ten to fifteen years ago, fathers weren't welcome in delivery rooms, and their participation in the birth process wasn't a possibility. A man was relegated to the hackneyed vignette of a distraught, unshaven father-to-be pacing the floor far from the action in the delivery room (the hallowed province of a woman and her obstetrician), waiting for the doctor to emerge and deliver his news like a presidential edict. That was for normal, uncomplicated deliveries.

Ten years ago, it would have been unthinkable to have

a father present in an operating room for delivery by cesarean section. Cesarean section is, after all, major surgery. But in 1980, a prestigious medical panel meeting at the National Institutes of Health, the government's major medical research organization, concluded that fathers should be present during cesarean section if possible (a well-placed screen usually hides the more graphic details from the husband's view). One of the recommendations of the panel went this way: "Hospitals are encouraged to liberalize their policies concerning the option of having the father or surrogate attend the cesarean birth." The panel also said, "The healthy neonate should not be routinely separated from mother and father following delivery," even if delivery must be by surgery. The medical community, which tends to be ultra-conservative, is recognizing that fathers are parents, too—and that is all to the good for babies as well as fathers.

One of the major reasons for fatherhood's emerging importance in early childhood research is logistical: it's simply a fact that more mothers are returning to work when their babies are still tiny. It used to be that a mother returned to work, if she did so at all, when her youngest child reached school age at five or six. Thus for many women who had had careers there was a span of ten years or more when they assumed the traditional role of caregiver to their children while the man went off to the office everyday.

In this kind of marriage there is evidence that men have budged little from traditional, stereotyped roles of masculine behavior. But in cases where a mother is working outside the home three months after the birth of the baby, the father's active participation in child-rearing usually becomes a necessity. Cesarean fathers often achieve a close, warm relationship with their babies very early because their wives are exhausted from surgery and must rest, notes

Beyond Bonding: Fathers Are Parents, Too

Frank A. Pedersen, research psychologist with the National Institute of Child Health and Human Development. Father's help isn't just a fringe benefit then—it's badly needed.

In a small study group of cesarean-delivered babies observed at five months of age, Pedersen found that their fathers were generally more responsive to them than were the fathers of babies delivered vaginally. This, he feels, was because the fathers got to know their babies earlier by caring for them more intensively in the first few weeks of the babies' lives. A cesarean father who discovers for himself the joys of stimulating and playing with a bright, healthy baby makes an excellent parent-teacher.

Fathers and Infant Signals

It's 3:00 A.M., and the baby's crying. Mother wakes up and looks through half-closed lids at Father, who's still sleeping soundly. Yawning and sighing, she swings her feet over the side of the bed, wiggles her toes into slippers, and walks down the hall to the nursery, where she picks the baby up from her crib. Father never stirs.

How true is this scenario? Of course it's true in some traditional households where the mother does most or all of the caregiving. It also seems to be true that—perhaps because female brains are oriented more toward words and sounds—mothers hear infant crying at night more readily than their husbands do.

But Michael Lamb and two other fatherhood researchers, Ross D. Parke and Ann M. Frodi, have found that the oblivious-father scenario simply doesn't hold up. In fact, they have found that fathers, when awake and alert, are generally just as responsive to infant signals as mothers. During feeding, for instance, Parke found that fathers were just as sensitive to the baby's coughing, sneezing, and spitting as mothers.

The fathers would stop feeding the baby, look at the infant carefully, and talk to the baby during coughing or spitting episodes. When the baby gurgled, fathers were especially sensitive to the infant's attempts at talking, and took care to talk back—even more than mothers. And in the true test of whether fathers are as sensitive to a baby's signals while feeding as a mother, Parke discovered by meticulous scientific measurement that the amount of milk consumed by a baby was about the same whether a father or mother fed the infant.

During feeding, mothers seemed more likely to touch their babies in response to the baby's gurgles, while fathers responded more readily with talking, not touching. Parke theorizes that fathers may be more hesitant to touch the baby during feeding because they're concerned about interrupting the feeding routine. It doesn't mean that fathers don't react to their babies just as sensitively as mothers, he concluded; they just react slightly differently. Both kinds of responses are fine for the baby.

Fathers and Infant Stimulation

In his fathering studies, Parke has found that the way mothers and fathers stimulate their babies shifts during the baby's first three months of life. When the baby is a newborn, fathers tend to stimulate them more than mothers—by showing them a toy and shaking it, for example. Later, when the baby is three months of age, mothers use this kind of stimulation a little more than fathers.

A similar shift occurs with routine caretaking, such as checking diapers and wiping the baby's face; mothers do more of this when the baby is a newborn, while fathers

Beyond Bonding: Fathers Are Parents, Too

play more of a role as the baby gets older. Parke feels what happens is that fathers and mothers learn from each other and borrow each other's behavior: mothers become more active stimulators and fathers take a more active role in routine caregiving as the baby grows older.

Researchers have found that in general American fathers' play styles are quite different from mothers' play styles. A father joyfully throws his infant up in the air, while both chuckle with delight. It's arousing, physically stimulating—not passive or intellectual. While Mother is more interested in play objects (toys, dolls), Father prefers the physical rough and tumble.

All of this isn't surprising when you consider that in general women are more verbal than men, and men tend to have a more developed sense of spatial relations. Who benefits from the different styles of stimulation? The baby, of course. Early verbal exploration with Mom helps to ready the child for language, while the roughhousing play with Dad gives the baby a sense of his body dimensions and physical capabilities. In his reactions to his new baby, Father is often more a doer than a thinker; he provides the interest and stimulus to try it, again and again, until it works—whatever it is. The introduction to a child's physical surroundings thus comes more logically from the father, who tends to be a left-brained, spatial manipulator of the world.

The learning-by-doing style of a baby and preschooler is ideally suited to the father's temperament. If the mother teaches a "let's think about it" attitude, born of a more contemplative, protective stance, the father teaches a "let's see what happens" attitude, born of a competitive drive to succeed. Both styles are necessary to deal with the different kinds of problems your child will face as he grows older. Of course these mother/father differences in play styles and ways of reacting to an infant are changing as families change. As more single parents become heads of households and play both roles, mother and father combined, cultural differences in the way mothers and fathers relate to their children will blur.

Boy Babies Get More Stimulation

In general, studies show, this frolicsome father/infant play is more vigorous with boys; and predictably, it affects boys' intellectual growth more during babyhood than it does that of girls.

Ross Parke has observed that fathers treat firstborn sons differently from daughters even in the newborn period. Regardless of outcries about the dangers of "pink and blue" sex stereotyping, these differences seem to have to do with the cultural bias that values a firstborn son as an heir. In one study, fathers touched firstborn boys in the hospital more than girls or second or third sons. Fathers talked more to firstborn male newborns than to firstborn girls. "Clearly, there may be some basis to the claim that fathers really do prefer boys—especially firstborn boys," Parke has concluded.

He notes that there has traditionally been a "my son, the doctor" syndrome on the part of fathers that tends to foster the intellectual growth of boys more than that of girls. This sometimes submerged belief may be why some fathers have encouraged their boys to be independent explorers of their environment and high academic achievers, while girls have been expected merely to be popular and have a good time.

Regardless of differences in how they stimulate and relate to their new babies by sex, fathers do, in fact, relate—and that's an important plus for a baby. In one study

Beyond Bonding: Fathers Are Parents, Too

the father assumed a more dominant role as his child's playmate as the child passed from infancy to toddlerhood. At fifteen months the child's main playmate was his mother, but by twenty months the mother and father shared this role.

Even in traditional homes where the father goes off to work every day and the mother stays home with the children, the father's clear preference for physical, stimulating play—especially with firstborn boys—seems to make him an important force in his baby's life, notes Michael Lamb. Although he may not be with his child all day, he seems to make up for it with some welcome rough-and-tumble games when he gets home.

If the father's rough-and-tumble play is lavished more vigorously on infant sons, his major influence on his daughter's intellectual growth seems to come later. Girls who develop a sense of self-reliance and independence often have strong, even abrasive altercations with their fathers; in other words, they learn to stand up to them and argue with them.

Fathers in Flux

Although most researchers agree that fathers are assuming an increasingly important role in their children's lives while they are still babies, getting a fix on just how important the father's role is as a stimulator of his child is difficult. Families are in a state of flux. Today some families have stepfathers, some have stepmothers, and some families are single-parent families with only a mother or a father. Just having the terminology to deal with the new families demands some ingenuity; terms that have been used to refer to such families include "nontraditional," "reconstituted," and "blended." The problem with some of these terms is that they sound as if they belong to orange juice, not people.

Semantics aside, what effect does all this reconstituting and blending have on children? Some studies have shown that children (especially boys) who are raised in families without a father don't do as well on IQ tests, don't achieve as much when they get to school, and don't form friendships with other children as readily as youngsters raised in families with fathers as well as mothers. These studies emphasize the importance of a father as an intellectual prod and social force in his children's lives. But it would be wrong to conclude from observing a few maladjusted fatherless children in research studies that all children with no father present are poorly adjusted and intellectually stunted. It's simply not true.

In homes where mothers are raising babies without fathers, it helps to have a second adult around to stimulate the children and give them companionship and love—a second adult who may be a man or a woman. If the second adult is a man, he can provide the frolicsome playtimes a father would, the touching, the rolling about on the floor, the joyful tosses up in the air with strong hands ready to accept small charges on the way down.

And the myth of the wicked stepfather—the male counterpart of Cinderella's acid-tongued persecutor—seems to be just that, a myth. Such a limited and hostile stereotypical view simply hasn't held up under the research scrutiny of anthropology professor Paul Bohannon. He has concluded that, in general, children living with stepfathers do just as well as children living with their natural fathers—and are just as happy.

What of the single parent who happens to be a father? Far from being a bumbler who can't fry an egg, do a load of wash, change a diaper, or give a child "mother love," a single father is usually a strong, competent individual who cares deeply for his children and will do everything he can to give them a good start, including providing them with stimulation time. If a single father is divorced, his competence can be assumed; if he weren't capable of raising a child, chances are he would not have custody. Child custody laws have traditionally favored mothers.

Fostering Fathering

If you're a father reading this and you're not a househusband, you may be thinking how tough it is to be your child's first teacher and pursue a career as well. But fathers are coming out of the office and into their children's lives, and as a result many avenues of support are finally beginning to open up for men who want to experience fatherhood fully and be there when their children are learning, growing, and exploring.

In addition to childbirth education classes and courses on parenting taught in schools, organizations like the 92nd Street Young Men's & Young Women's Hebrew Association in New York City are beginning to offer specific courses on fatherhood. The New York Y started a course called "Fatherhood: The Pleasures and Pains," and a second called "Fatherhood After the Break: Parenting Alone." The Y also started a new play group specifically for fathers and their toddlers on Sundays; it's called Park Bench. "We realized it was kind of discriminatory not to include fathers," said a Y staffer of the decision to start a play group for fathers and their children. Your area may offer similar courses and programs, or you might think about helping to get them started.

Traditionally, companies have been fairly hard-nosed about their hours and the kind of time commitment they require from workers, but that time-clock mentality is changing. More and more companies are instituting flextime policies, allowing employees to set their own hours, which seem to work just fine. A man who can set his own hours at work can leave later in the morning, thus giving himself time to change, dress, feed, and play with a baby, or have breakfast and play with a toddler.

Alternatively, a man on flextime who functions well in the early morning can leave work earlier in the day and have the late afternoon with his children. Many early-bird workers say they get more done if they go to work at, say, 7:00 A.M., because their phones aren't ringing off the hook and they aren't constantly being interrupted. Flextime workers often report that they feel less conflict between home and work responsibilities—and that goes for men as well as women.

Job sharing is another way to provide men with more time for fathering. On some American college campuses, a husband and wife, each with a doctoral degree in the same field, share a single faculty position, thus giving each more time at home with their children. These couples say they not only have better relationships with their children, but—as an extra dividend—closer, warmer relationships with each other.

In addition to groups like Parents Without Partners, specifically male support groups are becoming established in cities like Philadelphia and New York. These groups give men a chance to meet with one another and talk over problems they share, including fathering issues.

Paternity Leave: Promises, Promises

Finally there is the matter of paternity leave. In 1974, a trail-blazing program called the Parental Insurance Plan was introduced to Sweden. The plan provides the parents of a new baby with up to nine months of paid leave that can be divided between them, as long as both aren't on full-time leave at the same time. Both can work half-time for nine months, or they can divide up the nine months so that, for example, the mother takes three months off, the father takes three months off, and then the mother takes three months off again. (The pay isn't full pay, amounting to about 90 percent of a parent's salary for the first six months after the baby's birth, and a minimum daily wage for the last three months.)

By all rights, Swedish fathers should be miles ahead of American fathers in becoming important parent-teachers in their babies' lives. At 90 percent of a full-time salary, a father on Swedish paternity leave can afford to take some time to stimulate, care for, and play with his baby while the baby is still very young. In fact, however, only about 5 percent of Swedish men take a month of paid leave, according to Michael Lamb, who has studied the Swedish system.

Even more surprising, however, were the results of Lamb's studies of Swedish fathers' importance in their young children's lives. Even when their fathers took care of them, Swedish babies clearly preferred their mothers. No matter how involved their fathers were in caring for them, the babies wanted to stay near, touch, gurgle to, and be held by their mothers.

Researcher Lamb found these results especially surprising since studies in the United States have shown that at eight months babies don't show a clear preference for either parent, and that at sixteen months they may actually prefer their fathers (especially boys). What does it all mean?

In general, Lamb found, Swedish mothers and fathers stimulated and played with their babies far less than American parents do. Swedish fathers were much more restrained in their play, and didn't exhibit the rollicking, roughhousing form of play that delights many American fathers and their babies. Thus, although the Swedish fathers may have been more involved in giving care—feeding, changing diapers—they may not have been giving the babies the kind of stimulation the babies themselves considered important.

"Conceivably, the playfulness of American fathers helps to make them more psychologically important to their youngsters, despite the limited amount of time they spend together," Michael Lamb wrote in an article for *Psychology Today* magazine. An American father's play style may, in fact, be more important to a baby's development than researchers have yet realized. The one person who seems to realize the importance of Father's play style is the American baby, whose ecstatic gurgles as she is being launched in the air or tumbled over on her back by a pair of strong hands say far more than fifty research articles.

More liberalized child-care leave for fathers is just beginning to become a reality in the United States, where traditional corporations have been slow to manipulate hours to suit the individual. Government employees at the U.S. Department of Labor recently bargained for—and won—child-care leave for both men and women for a period of up to two years. In an agreement reached in July 1980, members of Local 12 of the American Federation of Government Employees (AFGE) persuaded management to

Beyond Bonding: Fathers Are Parents, Too

allow married or unmarried men or women to take a combination of annual leave and leave without pay to raise young children.

AFGE made it clear that this was to be child-care leave, not "maternity" or "paternity" leave. "We wanted to make the point that raising children is an equal burden for fathers and mothers," commented Local 12 president Bettejane Lumpkin shortly after the victory. What she did not add is that raising children can also be an equal joy for fathers and mothers.

Researchers still have much to learn from American babies about why they find fathers so stimulating and so exciting. Is it the physical sensations of flying through the air, feeling skin on skin a little roughly, or rolling on the floor? Is it the sense of being just slightly out of control but knowing someone's there to catch you so it's all right? How do all these sensations help the baby develop? Do they strengthen the nervous system? Build up the muscles? Quicken the reflexes? Fuel a sense of self-confidence and competence?

Although all the answers to these intriguing questions aren't yet known, it is clear that Father is emerging as an important developmental force in his children's lives, starting when they are still babies. Most fathers, and most mothers, too, would respond unhesitatingly, "It's about time."

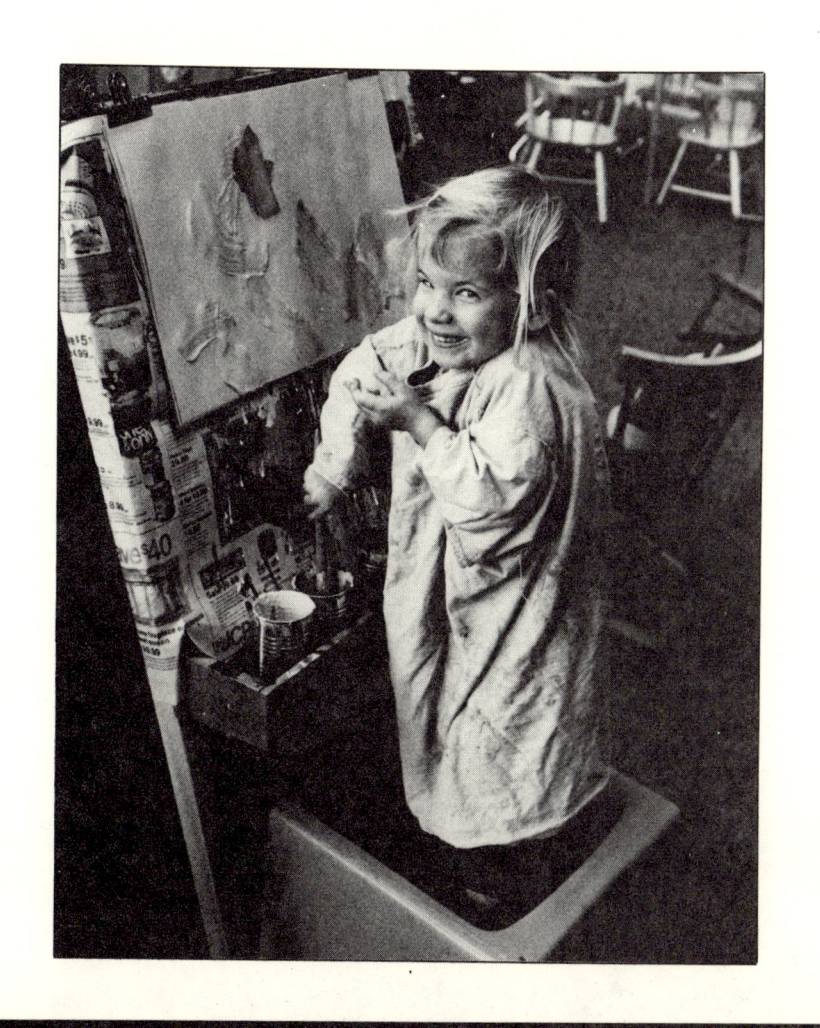

11. Early Learning: Where Do We Go from Here?

> Research on the intellectual development of the child highlights the fact that at each stage of development the child has a characteristic way of viewing the world and explaining it to himself. The task of teaching a subject to a child at any particular age is one of representing the structure of that subject in terms of the child's way of viewing things.
>
> —JEROME S. BRUNER, *The Process of Education*

In the last two decades, we have learned from researchers that indeed our children are much smarter than we think, and at a much earlier age. Babies only a few months old can focus their eyes on objects and study them. They respond to their parents' talking by listening and trying to "talk back" themselves. They stick out their tongues when an adult does, in an uncanny facial imitation of "Pooh on you!" Babies and young children are, in short, brilliant learners—absorbing and quickly assimilating a daunting array of new sights, sounds, and signals.

The only comparable situation for an adult to what a child learns would be suddenly awaking to find oneself on a strange planet and having to make one's way among gigantic, odd-looking inhabitants who speak a strange language. Add to that having to learn to walk all over again and maybe we can gain an inkling of the learning challenge babies face.

What do we do with the new knowledge we have gained about out children's early intelligence and rapid development? What implications does this knowledge have for our child care and educational systems, and do we want to do anything about those implications? What can we do to ensure that our children have the very best learning opportunities, but aren't pushed to acquire knowledge that's not framed in their own terms?

Who Will Raise the Children?

There are some child development experts who now say that because the first few years of life are so crucial to a child's development, parents simply cannot bow out and turn the job of raising a child over to another caregiver, no matter how competent. One of these is Burton White, who readily concedes that his position is unpopular with working women.

"Nothing a young mother or father does out of the home is more important or rewarding than raising a baby" is how he himself views his stand. White, who as director of the Center for Parent Education in Newton, Massachusetts, views himself as a child advocate, takes the position that it is not best for a baby to be placed in full-time substitute care, and he must advocate what is best for babies.

Barring certain situations—cases of families with serious alcohol or drug abuse problems or tragic cases where the family simply doesn't want the job of giving a baby a good start—White believes the baby is better off with his parents. He bends to recommend part-time substitute care for parents who want it. And he concedes that Mother doesn't have to do it all—that caring fathers and grandparents make excellent "mothers" for babies and young children. Nevertheless, White's position is hard for many working mothers to accept.

If you are a working mother reading this, you may be disturbed by the thought that you are somehow harming your baby's development if you go back to work several months after the baby is born and continue to work during the baby's first years of life. Such feelings provide only a source of guilt for women who have worked hard to develop careers or attain certain positions and would lose ground if they took years off to raise a child.

More important, such feelings aren't supported by the results of research studies, which show that paid maternal employment has no harmful effects on the growth and development of the child or on family life in general—except under certain unusual conditions. In 1973, Mary C. Howell, a physician who is a former associate dean for student affairs at Harvard Medical School, surveyed published research studies to see what effect, if any, a mother's working had on her child. She could find no indication that the mother's employment per se made any real difference when it came to the child's sense of competence, self-esteem, or achievement in learning tasks.

In the spring of 1984, Howell, who is also trained as a developmental psychologist, again surveyed published research studies on the effect of a mother's employment on her child. After carefully examining thirty-seven published studies that had been done since 1973, Howell again concluded that there is no evidence that mothers' employment harms their children. In fact, she believes that both working and nonworking mothers actually spend about the same amount of concentrated time with their children, and the only real difference is that working mothers are not instantly available to their children at all hours. She further believes that working can enhance mothering because it can: foster flexibility in the mother that allows her to adapt as her child grows and changes, eventually letting go as the child seeks independence; help the child develop self-esteem by a positive osmosis, since those who have high esteem can transmit that quality to others; lead to the honesty in relationships that is essential for children to experience. "Employment helps you know yourself" is how Howell puts this last point.

Mary Howell, who is the mother of six, believes that mothers themselves are the best judges of when they can and should return to work after the birth of a child. "My own reading of the literature is that the mother should remain a full-time caretaker as long as she feels the intense bond between her child and herself cannot be diluted," she told an auditorium of primarily working women at a conference called "The Professional Woman as Mother," sponsored by three medical groups in Washington, D.C.

The decision to return to work is indeed one the mother herself should make, unburdened by guilt she does not deserve. If you're working, you know your decision depends on a number of factors: how much you need the money; how much you would feel personally devastated by losing ground in your chosen field; how your spouse feels about your working; how much you really want to become a full-time caregiver of your baby; and what kind of support help you can get to help you raise your baby in the way that you would like him to be raised.

The important point is that we now know babies need certain kinds of loving stimulation above and beyond mere feeding when they're hungry and diaper changing when they're wet to develop their abilities and creativity. Without that conscious stimulation—physical, verbal, visual—your baby will not learn about her environment as rapidly as she can. Therefore, if for any number of reasons you elect to return to work soon after your baby is born and to leave your child with someone else, make sure that someone else would do things as nearly your way as possible. Just as parents tend to reflect the quality of care they had when they were children, so substitute caregivers tend to

Early Learning: Where Do We Go from Here?

give the same kind of care to children they were given when they were small. For this reason it's important to try to find out something about the early background of the person you're considering hiring. In a tactful conversation, you can try to find out if the prospective caregiver's early years were happy ones, and whether she (or he) felt loved and received the one-on-one kind of attention you want for your child. It's not difficult to interpret answers to discreet questions about someone's early childhood. James H. Egan, chairman of the Department of Psychiatry at Children's Hospital National Medical Center in Washington, D.C., puts it this way: "If you say 'Tell me a little about your background' and the person gives a demonic denunciation of her mother, then you can say 'Thank you very much.'" And send the applicant on her way.

Studies have shown that the more verbal dexterity a child learns at home by repeating and using sounds, the faster and more easily he will learn to read in school (see Chapter Three). If you're considering a caregiver whose native language is not English, remember that your baby will learn language by imitating what he hears. While in theory it might be delightful to have a bilingual child, in practice you confuse the learning process by asking your baby to learn two sets of sounds—one from his caregiver during the day and one from you in the evenings and on weekends. While there aren't any rules on this, consider that you're in effect asking your baby to do double duty in learning to speak. It is far wiser to find someone who speaks English and will talk to your baby in that language, enunciating clearly and distinctly so that the baby can hear the sounds he will eventually use every day as his native tongue.

Is the person you're considering hiring a happy, outgoing, and curious person? If not, she or he may not be as responsive to your baby's early explorations and tentative learning attempts as you would like. Does the person think in terms of "baby-sitting"—literally sitting in front of the TV or talking on the phone while the baby does his own thing, on his own? Does the person have a sense of how intelligent and curious babies are and how much they can learn, or does he or she think of the baby as a little doll who needs only to eat, sleep, and be changed when he cries? If you talk to the person about infant stimulation, will you draw a blank? Or will the person respond by indicating she knows how bright, alert, and educable babies really are?

If you have already hired someone and she is staying with your child, does she excitedly tell you what your child did that day when you come home? Or does she respond to your questions about the baby's activity with few words, and stick to the necessary aspects of caregiving: how much the baby ate, how often she had to change him, how long he slept, whether he was fussy and cried.

The cost of quality child care (in the sense of the curious, loving, stimulating person described above) is expensive, as is the cost of any important service. If you're paying for the service, you have a right to something more than mere custodial care. And, most important, your child has a right to more than custodial care no matter what you're paying. You might want to consider doing something from your home or working part-time so that you minimize your time away from home and your child care expenses. The concept of "flexiplace"—an office at home or a satellite office near where you live—is becoming much more workable with sophisticated computer technology, such as video display terminals hooked up to the main headquarters of a corporation.

Preschools: What Is Quality Time?

Sooner or later in your child's development, you'll probably start shopping in your community for a "quality" daycare center or preschool. Even though parents are their children's first and most important teachers, many mothers and fathers want some help with the job when their children are three or four, before they go to kindergarten.

In addition to helping children learn thinking skills and creative ways of using their hands (drawing and cutting, for example), good preschools are excellent places for children to learn how to get along with others. A good preschool may be your child's first introduction to a world that doesn't revolve around him (or his second introduction, if there are older children at home). A good preschool prepares your child for the new world of kindergarten and gives him an adjustment edge over children who've had no preschool.

Unfortunately for bewildered parents looking for a quality preschool, there's a wide array of U.S. day-care centers ranging from mediocre to excellent, with a lot falling into the in-between category. But there are certain objective standards parents can use to judge what kind of day-care center is likely to be a good learning experience for their children, not just a group baby-sitting experience.

Results from the 1979 final report of the National Day Care Study, which looked at quality issues in day-care centers subsidized by the federal government, make clear what those standards are. For the first time, this study showed that children do better in language and thinking and social skills and score higher on standardized tests such as the Preschool Inventory (PSI) and the revised Peabody

Picture Vocabulary Test (PPVT) when they attend preschools with certain characteristics.

What's the success formula? It is small groups of children supervised by caring adults with specific training in child development and early childhood education. The emphasis on small group size turns out to be more important than the number of staff per children in the center. Groups of 12 to 14 children with two caregivers scored higher on standardized tests than groups of 24 to 28 children with four adult staffers, for instance.

The child–staff ratio wasn't totally unimportant, but it turned out to be a factor of less importance than overall group size—along with the philosophy of the staff, and the amount of indoor and outdoor space available per child. Specifically, the National Day Care Study showed that children do better in smaller groups because:

- The primary teachers do less passive observation of children and more roll-up-the-sleeves play alongside them.
- Children talk more, cooperate better, and show more initiative and leadership.
- The children show fewer signs of hostility and inner conflict and don't wander aimlessly about the room, showing a lack of interest in the center's activities.
- Children learn to use their brains more intensively, as evidenced by scores on the PSI and PPVT.
- The primary teachers devote less of their time to herding, managing, and ordering the children to do things and more of their time participating in activities and social relations with the children.

None of this is very surprising, of course. Anyone with even a smidgeon of knowledge about how young children learn could have predicted the findings of this study be-

Early Learning: Where Do We Go from Here?

fore it was even done. Anyone who's ever worked in a day-care center could have told you what the study results would say. But what is surprising, and distressing, is that states seem to be ignoring the news. There is a wide variation from state to state in licensing laws on crucial issues such as group size and whether a professional child development associate (CDA) credential or bachelor's degree is required of day-care staffers.

Raymond C. Collins, director of program development in the Office of Developmental Services of the federal Administration for Children, Youth and Families, recently compared child-care licensing requirements for four-year-olds in the fifty states, the District of Columbia, Guam, Puerto Rico, and the Virgin Islands. What he found was disturbing: "It would appear that states have paid little heed to the child-care research. Neither the findings that point toward improved child outcomes nor those that highlight favorable cost-quality trade-offs have been acted upon by most states." In other words, we know what works, but we're not doing it.

In 1981, thirty-three states, Guam, Puerto Rico, and the Virgin Islands had no specific requirements on group size for four-year-olds. In the remaining twenty-one states and the District of Columbia—where there were group size requirements—the range was appallingly large: a low of 10 children (very good) to a high of 45 children (impossible even with a high teacher–child staff ratio).

Only ten states and the District of Columbia required a B.S. or B.A. degree for at least one category of child-care staff in 1981. Of the ten, only three states specified that the degree had to be in early childhood education or child development. Worse, fourteen of the twenty-one states that had bachelor degree requirements in 1978 had dropped them by 1981, according to Collins' study. Only three states had actually tightened their academic requirements for child-care center staffers.

But, in a more hopeful vein, nine of the fourteen states that had dropped the academic bachelor's degree requirement had shifted to the less academic but skill-oriented CDA credential, and two more states had plans to include the CDA credential in their regulations. In all, Collins found, data available through April 1983 indicated that twenty-six states and the District of Columbia had adopted the CDA requirement into their regulations for at least one category of child-care center staff. An additional seven states had written the CDA credential into new draft regulations. More than 10,000 people now hold the CDA, which is granted by the federally supported CDA National Credentialing Program. CDA holders are caregivers who have demonstrated their skills in working with young children by completing requirements of the CDA credential award system. CDA holders don't have to have college degrees, but they have to understand child development.

Credentialing of individual workers aside, not all day-care centers in the country are licensed by the state in which they operate; in fact, church-affiliated child-care centers are specifically exempt from licensing. State and local licensing requirements unfortunately too often focus on the mechanical or logistical (how many bathrooms there are) without trying to evaluate what kind of educational experience a child is getting. But while licensing is hardly a guarantee that a child-care center will be a) safe, or b) learning-intensive, and while states vary greatly in their licensing requirements, at least licensing (or meeting licensing requirements without actually being licensed) is a baseline for child-care centers from which concerned parents can start.

Early Learning: Where Do We Go from Here?

The National Association for the Education of Young Children (NAEYC), a professional nonprofit association of some 38,000 early childhood educators, is currently in the process of developing voluntary national credentialing standards for child-care centers. Soon it may be possible for parents to ask center staff whether a particular child-care center is NAEYC-credentialed.

Where Are Our Priorities?

But problems in providing quality early-childhood education to our children go far beyond the issue of licensing or credentialing. The entire thrust of this book has been to show that our children are smarter than we think—and that they learn more, faster, as babies and preschoolers than they will ever learn again in their entire lives. That is the unmistakable message from an impressive and growing body of child development research.

If we listen to the researchers and accept the message, then we have a responsibility to do something about its implications—as a society, not just as individual parents. What are we doing about it? Perversely, we seem determined to ignore the message, if we look at the following facts:

• Preschool teachers, even those with solid academic credentials, are at the very bottom of the economic and social-status ladder in teaching, a notoriously underpaid profession. Many preschool teachers are lucky to take home ten thousand dollars a year—and must do without fringe benefits—vacation, pensions, and sick leave—common in other fields. Men supporting families cannot afford to be preschool teachers; only women with husbands who partially support them can really afford to be in the field.

Preschool teachers educate individuals when they are in

their prime learning years and when what they learn can determine what they will do with the rest of their lives. College and graduate school professors, who teach students whose tastes, abilities, study habits, and personalities have already been formed and developed, have the highest economic and social status in the teaching profession.

• Aside from a few federally supported programs for disadvantaged preschoolers such as Head Start, relatively little taxpayers' money is spent to educate preschoolers.

• Many of our day-care centers are not centers of learning; they are places of custodial care where a child can be dropped off and loosely supervised for the convenience of parents who have other things to do.

• Even accepting the fact that our child-care centers lack uniform standards of quality, there are not enough day-care slots for all the children in the country whose parents want them. This means there are not enough day-care centers, period, let alone centers of excellence where learning is prized and fostered.

While it would be foolhardy and irresponsible to take taxpayers' money away from secondary education and funnel it into preschool education, if more money were spent for quality preschool education for more children, more youngsters would enter first grade prepared for twelve years of academic learning. Somewhere along the line they are not getting that preparation, as evidenced by the generally mediocre performance of American high-schoolers in the aggregate. If the statistics on performance in high schools show anything, they show what happens to children who never develop a sense of the joy of learning and the pride that comes with mastering facts and concepts.

The National Commission on Excellence in Education,

a blue-ribbon group which exhaustively studied American education for eighteen months before making its report, *A Nation at Risk*, concluded that the nation's high schools are wastelands of mediocrity. In unusually strongly worded language for a government-appointed group, the commission concluded that "More and more young people emerge from high school ready neither for college nor for work." The statistics commission members gathered bear them out. They include these dismal findings:

• On nineteen academic tests comparing American students with students from other industrialized nations, the Americans were never first or second, and were last seven times.

• In a country that prides itself on providing a public education to all its citizens, some twenty-three million Americans are illiterate.

• About 13 percent of all seventeen-year-old Americans (who are normally in their last year of high school) can be considered functionally illiterate. Among minority teenagers, that figure may run as high as 40 percent.

• The average achievement of high-school students on most standardized tests is lower now than it was twenty-six years ago, during the Sputnik boom.

• More than half of the American students who are considered gifted (as measured by intelligence tests) aren't working up to their capacity, as measured by their performance on achievement tests.

• From 1963 to 1980, scores on the College Board's Scholastic Aptitude Tests (SAT) declined steadily. Verbal scores dropped an average of 50 points, while mathematics scores dropped nearly 40 points.

• Many seventeen-year-olds simply don't possess the intellectual reasoning powers we should expect of them.

Nearly 40 percent can't draw inferences (logical conclusions) from something they have read. Only one-fifth can write a persuasive essay. And only one-third can solve a mathematics problem that requires several steps in the thinking process.

• Corporate and military leaders are forced to spend millions of dollars on expensive remedial education courses for their personnel in such basic skills as reading, writing, spelling, and math. The Department of the Navy told the commission that fully 25 percent of its recruits can't read at even the ninth-grade level.

And on and on. The commission's findings, which have been largely supported by other recent educational study groups, heap doom on gloom. But things aren't dismal, especially for concerned parents. Read on in the next chapter to find out how to make sure your child gets a head start on learning, so that when she is older, the love of learning will be so ingrained that studying will be less of a chore and more of a joy. A child who is turned on to learning very early will be more likely to stay "on" in elementary, junior high, and high school.

Child Care: The Choice Is Yours

Sooner or later you'll probably face the issue of child care, either part-time or full-time. The choice will be easier for you if you think in terms of trying to give your child an enriching educational experience instead of mere babysitting. Obviously you want your child to be loved by a caring caregiver, but you also want her to learn during the precious years when learning takes place more rapidly than it ever will again.

The only way to determine what kind of child care is

Early Learning: Where Do We Go from Here?

best for your child is to visit a facility ahead of time. When visiting a preschool, make sure it meets all fire, safety, and licensing requirements in your community, and then look for the following:

1. Do the children seem to be moving around chaotically, or is there a daily schedule with goals and planned activities?

2. Do the teachers seem harried and frazzled, or are they able to spend time with individual children, sitting and helping them put in a wayward puzzle piece or cut with blunt scissors?

3. Do the teachers seem genuinely interested in helping children do things in individual ways, or is every child expected to copy a method and do it the same way?

4. Are coloring books used or is the child encouraged to draw his world freely the way he sees it?

5. Is the schedule divided between outdoor free play and quiet indoor play?

6. Is there a story time when the teacher reads to the children? Does she or he pause to let the children ask questions or make comments about the story during the reading?

7. Does the child have any choice about what he does when? For example, are there free playtimes when the child can choose whether to play with blocks or with the dollhouse?

8. Are children encouraged to do things for themselves under supervision—putting on their coats, washing their hands?

9. Equipment doesn't have to be fancy, but are there enough

- blocks;
- puzzles;

- dolls and stuffed animals;
- pieces of climbing equipment such as jungle gyms and slides;
- child-sized furniture, such as tables and chairs;
- art materials, such as construction paper, blank newsprint, crayons (every child should have a box with his name on them), blunt scissors;
- books?

10. Are there permanent or visiting animals (such as hamsters or guinea pigs) or growing plants for the children to watch?

11. Do staff members encourage the children to talk freely to communicate their needs, rather than hitting or crying to get what they want? Does the staff take the time to stop and listen while a child tries to say what he needs or what is bothering him?

12. Does the play space seem to be spacious enough for children's play, or do they keep bumping into each other? (As a good rule of thumb, the National Association for the Education of Young Children recommends that there be at least 35 square feet of usable playroom floor space inside per child and 75 square feet per child outside; if the center is licensed, ask the preschool director to give you her or his figures on play space per child.)

12. Conclusion: Toward a Learning Society

The problems with our educational system begin very early, long before a child has even started formal schooling. Not enough of our babies and young children are getting the kind of learning-intensive experiences—at their own level—that turn them into curious, creative individuals who thirst for knowledge in elementary, junior high, and high school. We believe that unless a baby's natural desire to learn is fostered, nurtured, valued, and otherwise handled as the precious commodity it is, the child can be turned off to learning, and thus to formal education.

In its report the National Commission on Excellence in Education apparently agreed with this view, at least in part. The commission had this word for parents: "As surely as you are your child's first and most influential teacher, your child's ideas about education and its significance begin with you. You must be a *living* example of what you expect your children to honor and to emulate. Moreover, you bear a responsibility to participate actively in your child's education." And the commission suggested to each parent that he or she "nurture your child's curiosity, creativity, and confidence; and be an active participant in the work of the schools. Above all, exhibit a commitment to continued learning in your own life." A tall order? Not for parents who believe that learning begins at home and never stops.

Israeli psychology professor Reuven Feuerstein suggests that parents view themselves as essential "mediators" between their children and the experiences their children have. In this way parents become caring coaches of the learning process. Being a mediator entails assuming responsibility for the child's learning, he points out; if the child fails, it is more a reflection on the mediator than it is on the child.

Feuerstein, who believes intelligence can be molded much as one molds clay, evolved his theory of mediated learning while working with children whom standard tests had branded as having low IQs, and who were considered slow learners. He is convinced that all children—from gifted to handicapped—can be helped to learn by being lovingly, carefully, and methodically coached. His testing sessions are more like tutorial sessions, and often last several hours. Feuerstein gives a student a learning task and coaches her until the child can complete the task. When that one's complete, the psychologist presents another, slightly more complex task, and so the tutorial proceeds in a coached-learning way until Feuerstein finds out what the student can learn (not what she does not know). The mediator in coached-learning sessions talks to the child encouragingly when he gets stuck, gives hints, and otherwise cajoles and coaxes the learning process along. It's very different from sitting alone at a desk with a piece of paper and a pencil, and it's something all concerned parents can do at home.

The Israeli psychologist was a student of Swiss psychologist Jean Piaget, whose ideas are threaded throughout this book. The implications of Feuerstein's work are far-reaching. What they boil down to is that children, even those considered slow learners, learn more readily when they are coached by someone who knows how to develop their thinking skills and cares enough to do it. Such a commitment should be the foundation of a society that wants children to learn.

The National Commission on Excellence in Education recommended that the United States embark on educa-

Conclusion: Toward a Learning Society

tional reform that has as its heart the creation of "a learning society." What's that? It's a philosophy, not a specific curriculum, and it starts when a child is still tiny. "At the heart of such a society is the commitment to a set of values and to a system of education that affords all members the opportunity to stretch their minds to full capacity, from early childhood through adulthood, learning more as the world itself changes," in the words of the commission report.

A learning society stresses *how* to learn as much as it stresses what is learned—the process of thinking as well as the end product of that brainwork. "In contrast to the ideal of the Learning Society . . . we find that for too many people education means doing the minimum work necessary for the moment, then coasting through life on what may have been learned in its first quarter." This damning statement was the conclusion of the commission's report about the loss of intellectual curiosity, the sense of wonder that is as natural to babies as eating.

In his book *The Process of Education,* Jerome S. Bruner takes the view that any subject can be taught to a child in an intellectually honest way at any stage of development, provided that the information is presented to the child in terms he can understand. What does this mean for preschoolers?

A preschool child is in what Piaget called the pre-operational stage. This is the stage during which the child is manipulating her world through action and learning through her senses. She pushes a ball; it rolls on the floor. Much later she may develop the skills of a crack bowler; for now she learns that round balls roll when you push them. If she tries to roll the ball uphill, she will note that it will come right back down, instead of continuing to roll up; this is her first lesson in gravity, and only one of a vast number of learning experiences for the pre-operational child. Without a great number of these physical action-oriented experiences, a preschool child will learn very little about the world around her.

As we've seen, the pre-operational child is very egocentric: when the sun sinks into the horizon it is going to sleep, just as she goes to sleep at night in her bed. But even at this stage it is possible to teach basic biology, for example. A preschool child who asks why his dog has a fuzzy coat can be told in simple terms that the heavy coat protects the dog from the cold, just as the child's winter coat protects him. If, among his why questions, he asks why he wears clothes and the dog doesn't, you can point out that the child has smooth skin over most of his body which lacks fur and that is why he needs the protection of warm clothes and the dog doesn't. This observation can lead him to observe other mammals with fur that don't need clothes, such as animals in the zoo.

A preschool child whose mother is expecting can be told that the baby will come from Mother's tummy, and that is why Mother's stomach is so large (he does not need clinical details about exactly where the baby will emerge). You can tell him that he, too, was once a tiny baby who grew in Mother's tummy, and that in fact all human babies come from a mother's tummy (no test-tube baby explanations are needed at this point).

Even more important than what you tell your child about natural phenomena is how you tell it. Try to transmit a sense of wonder and excitement to your child. Isn't it absolutely marvelous that his dog grows such a fine, thick coat to protect him against chilly winter winds and snow? In this way you're fueling your child's sense of wonder and enthusiasm about learning with your own sense of wonder. Wonder is contagious.

Conclusion: Toward a Learning Society

The best learning experiences for a preschool child are often spontaneous, not programmed. That is one reason why flash cards are hardly an ideal method of teaching preschoolers anything. When your child drops to the ground to observe a flower more closely, do you drop to the ground with him, smile, and remark on the beautiful shape and colors of the flower? Or do you hurry the child along, worrying about getting to the supermarket and ignoring the flower and yet another valuable learning opportunity? The best time for learning is when your child is excited, curious, transfixed by something he sees, hears, or touches.

All of this sounds pretty utopian. Letting a child experience learning at his own pace, in his own way, doesn't really jibe with classroom learning, where all the children sit at desks and do basically the same tasks, which are chosen by the teacher, not the children. How we can restructure our public elementary schools to promote more effective learning is the subject of another book.

But what we do know is that preschools can be structured to make the most of the way a child learns naturally. In this way a good preschool can be a bridge between the free play of babyhood and the structured classroom learning of elementary school.

The best kind of preschool, no matter what it's called, is a preschool that values the teaching of Piaget. A Piagetian preschool has been called a "developmental classroom," but by any name it's simply a place where the teacher determines the child's level of skills and readiness to learn more. A Piagetian preschool shuns flash cards and early reading. Rather, the school values your child's degree of body awareness (see the section on whole-body learning at the end of Chapter Three), and regards body awareness and movement as essential tools for learning. A child must be physically as well as mentally ready to learn. This kind of preschool values your child's readiness to learn different skills, and doesn't try to superimpose facts on the child before she's ready to comprehend what they mean.

The best preschool tunes in to your child's physical as well as mental readiness for learning. Can your two- or three-year-old child put her hand on her nose when you ask her to find it? Can she find the top of her body? The bottom? Can she roll on the floor? Lie on her stomach and lift first a leg, then the other leg, then each arm in turn? Both arms at once? Both legs at once? If you draw a slightly wavy line across a piece of paper, can she carefully and slowly tear it with her hands quite close to the line? A preschool that values the development of your child takes note of all these factors, recognizing that your child learns through her senses.

This kind of school provides materials so a child can learn at her own pace and readiness level: paints, clay, sand, blocks of various sizes, puzzles with different degrees of difficulty. The school provides some structure and has a schedule, but also respects and values a child's need for free play with other children. "The educator provides, the child decides" is how Hans G. Furth and Harry Wachs, co-authors of *Thinking Goes to School,* put it.

Furth and Wachs examine Piaget's theory in practice and point out that if the level of a task or problem is too high for a bright, normal child, he'll ignore it or manipulate it into something he can handle with the skills he already has mastered. This is the psychologically healthy reaction of a child who hasn't yet reached the level of readiness needed to handle a particular task (such as reading or writing his name), and who knows it.

When you go shopping for a good preschool, it's not necessary to ask the teachers whether it's a "Piagetian

Conclusion: Toward a Learning Society

preschool." The school might be exactly that without the teachers really knowing the terminology. Instead, observe how the teachers work (and play) with the children. Do they seem rigidly to insist that all the children do exactly the same thing at the same time? Are they sticklers for commonly accepted ways of doing things, instead of the unconventional and individual solution? Do they value creativity and artistic expression, or only the ability to tie a shoe or write a name?

If a child colors the sky pale yellow, does the teacher send him back and tell him the sky is blue and to "do it right"? Or does she remark on the beautiful yellow sky and say the sun must be shining brightly to make it that color? If a child makes a dog with wings out of clay, does the teacher express dismay and send him back to "do it right" because everyone knows dogs don't have wings? Or does she exclaim over the fascinating creature that can not only run along the ground on its paws sniffing with its nose but also take off and skim over the clouds like an airplane?

Your child's curiosity, sense of wonder, personal creativity, freedom of expression, motivation to learn, and joyous assimilation of the world can be cultivated and nurtured in a preschool situation—or squashed. Why not try to nurture your child's unique intelligence early? Why not try to cultivate a creative, thinking individual, not another conformist?

How do we know this kind of nurturing works? Do effective preschools that value a child's intellect, individuality, and creativity really work? How do we know they make a difference? The very best evidence derives from what has come to be known as the Perry Preschool Program, in Ypsilanti, Michigan.

In 1962 David P. Weikart, who was then director of special services for the Ypsilanti public school system, received local and state funds (the program later received federal funding) to set up and run a daily preschool program for children who seemed destined for failure because of the economic and social strikes against them.

These children were "disadvantaged"—their families were undereducated and underemployed, and there weren't a lot of extra resources to help the developing preschoolers exercise their brainpower. The children were selected in part because they came from families that lived at the poverty level; these were, in short, poor children, all of whom happened to be black. The study of these first preschoolers was originally designed to test a simple hypothesis: that early educational intervention in a child's life has a positive effect.

In a report co-authored with Lawrence J. Schweinhart, Weikart—who is now president of the nonprofit High/Scope Educational Research Foundation—summed up the philosophy of the Perry Preschool Program as a way of helping a child develop innate talents and abilities that were already there. As a person goes through life, the authors said, he is exposed to many influences, experiences, and people, all helping to shape what the child will be: high in self-esteem or fearing failure, or somewhere in between. The child will perform, achieve, and assume a role according to what he learns he can do in the world very early; others will respond to him according to how he plays that role throughout his life.

"The individual maintains this role from the inside; teachers, parents, and peers communicate expectations which maintain the individual in this role from the outside. While change in this role is possible, it is extremely difficult; better to begin with a role conducive to success. Preschool represents a period of time when such a role may

Conclusion: Toward a Learning Society

be constructed through a high-quality educational program," wrote the researchers.

The Perry Preschool Program is important because we know not only what happened to the children in the short term, but also in the long term. Weikart has followed the 123 children in the study up through age fifteen to determine what effect the preschool education had on them when they got to public school. In the short term, children in the preschool showed immediate gains on tests that measure thinking ability and achievement. After one year of preschool, the children's IQs had risen on the average of 12 points per child when compared with children from similar family backgrounds who didn't have this preschool education.

In the long term, the preschool education decreased the number of students placed in special education or held back (retained in the same grade for another year). In the group of children from the Perry project, only 17 percent of the children needed such special remedial efforts by fourth grade, as compared with 38 percent of a group of children with similar backgrounds who didn't have preschool education.

The children from the Perry Preschool were considered more highly motivated by their teachers than children who didn't attend the preschool, and that sense of motivation continued through age fifteen. More of the fifteen-year-olds in the Perry group had thought of going to college (77 percent) than a group of similar non-Perry youngsters (60 percent). And—this is a very important barometer—65 percent of the Perry youngsters enjoyed talking with their parents about school when they reached fifteen, compared with only 33 percent of a comparable group of non-Perry fifteen-year-olds. Weikart and Schweinhart regarded students' willingness to do homework as evidence of their commitment to school at age fifteen, reasoning that actually *doing* homework is more a reflection of student motivation than teacher assignment of homework. Apparently, preschool education increased the students' willingness to do homework. In interviews, fully 68 percent of the Perry teen-agers said their school studies required homework, compared with only 40 percent of the non-Perry youngsters.

It's true that the Perry Preschool Program was designed for poor children. But the point is that the program shows that children's positive experience with early learning sticks. They may not all grow up to be high-level achievers, but they do place a much higher value on education for its own sake. Other studies and overviews of existing preschool programs support this view.

The government's Head Start preschool program for disadvantaged youngsters, born in the antipoverty era of the 1960s, was discredited for a time by a national study called the Westinghouse report that found the benefits from Head Start fade away. But critics said the Westinghouse evaluation was riddled with problems in its methods and statistics-gathering techniques. Head Start, which is actually a collection of some two thousand programs nationally, has gotten better marks more recently from the Consortium for Longitudinal Studies, a group of twelve independent researchers.

In an overview report on Head Start research since 1970, the government found that almost all studies on Head Start children showed that their IQs tested higher than non-Head Start children of similar backgrounds on standard tests. Some—but not all—studies have shown that the Head Start children were able to maintain this advantage well into elementary school. Head Start usually improves the language development of preschool children, according to the research review, even though Head Start children aren't as verbal as middle-class children (whose parents presumably talk and read to them more than do disadvantaged parents).

One measure of Head Start's success is that it has remained truly sacred with Congress for some twenty years; during times of wholesale budget slashing for other federal programs, Head Start has kept its funding intact.

Obviously we need to shift our educational priorities so that we support more quality preschools. But it is absurd to suggest that a good preschool can do the complete job of educating your child for the world in which he will have to find his way. It can't. No preschool is a substitute for loving, concerned parents. In fact, the message from studies on effective preschool programs is that they work better when parents participate in them in some way.

As important as the daily preschool sessions for Perry children were home visits to the children and their mothers by preschool staffers for one and a half hours each week. These visits helped mothers understand the "home as school" concept (see Chapter Seven) and come to accept themselves as their children's most important teachers. A good preschool can hardly compensate for a home environment that is destructive to learning, and that was exactly the point of the home visits.

"In an immediate sense, parent involvement means that the child's environment is affected generally rather than in the one specific context of the preschool program," point out Yale University researchers Edward Zigler and Winnie Berman in an article on the future of early childhood education published in *American Psychologist,* a journal of the American Psychological Association. In other words, a preschool program that involves parents has an important ripple effect that permeates the child's total environment.

No matter what you choose to do about your child's preschool education, remember that you are an indispensable part of your child's learning. Your role in this educational process will continue throughout your child's life, but it will never be more important than it is from babyhood through the preschool years.

Your child is a great deal smarter than you think. It will be your privilege as a parent to discover just how bright, able, creative, and curious your youngster really is. Giving your child the psychological and emotional environment in which to learn, and reinforcement when he does, is the greatest gift, along with love, that you can give.

There is no adventure quite as exciting as helping your child develop unique capacities that are already there. And there is no process of discovery more stimulating than finding out what mysteries and treasures exist in your child's brain.

Best of all, there can be no more joyous or personally satisfying role than being your child's first and most important teacher.

Appendix
Information, Please: Resources for Parents

American Speech–Language–Hearing Association
10801 Rockville Pike
Rockville, Maryland 20852

Provides booklets and pamphlets on hearing, speech, and language in infants and young children; will provide referrals to hospital-, school-, or university-based speech/language/hearing clinics and programs in different parts of the country.

Association of Junior Leagues
825 Third Avenue
New York, New York 10022

The Junior League, through regional chapters in a national association of women volunteers, sponsors programs and centers on parent education around the country. Write for more information.

Center for Parent Education
55 Chapel Street
Newton, Massachusetts 02160

Directed by early childhood educator Burton L. White, the center publishes a newsletter and offers training institutes for professionals.

Council for National Cooperation in Aquatics, Inc.
P.O. Box 4724
Evansville, Indiana 47711

Write for information on infant swimming classes and specific safety guidelines for teaching such classes; CNCA supports swimming classes for preschoolers if these classes stress safety factors.

Family Focus/Family Resource Coalition
230 North Michigan Avenue
Suite 1625
Chicago, Illinois 60601

The coalition is a grass-roots federation of community-based family resource programs in the United States and Canada whose newsletter highlights such programs as the Minnesota Early Learning Design (MELD), a Minneapolis-based program that teaches skills and provides information to first-time parents.

Head Start Bureau
Office of Human Development Services
Administration for Children, Youth and Families
U.S. Department of Health and Human Services
P.O. Box 1182
Washington, D.C. 20013

Head Start is the government-funded preschool program started in 1965 for low-income preschoolers; since that year it has served more than eight million children. Write for general information and a booklet called "What Head Start Means to Families," which stresses the importance of parent involvement in the Head Start program.

Appendix: Information, Please: Resources for Parents

High/Scope Educational Reserach Foundation
High/Scope Press
600 North River Street
Ypsilanti, Michigan 48197

Founded by preschool educator David P. Weikart, the foundation publishes *High/Scope Resource*, a magazine for educators, and numerous books on the development of preschoolers; offers training institutes for professionals.

Home and School Institute
Special Projects Office
Suite 228
1201 16th Street, N.W.
Washington, D.C. 20036

This educational institute, founded in 1964, seeks to strengthen ties between school (including preschool) and home; it sponsors meetings and training institutes. Write for a list of publications.

Infant Stimulation Education Association
University of California—Los Angeles Center for Health Sciences
Factor 5-942
Los Angeles, California 90024

Founded by Susan M. Ludington, a nurse-educator, the association promotes tools and techniques to stimulate babies so they will develop to their full potential. ISEA sells tapes on infant stimulation, along with toys designed to stimulate growing babies.

Lekotek
613 Dempster
Evanston, Illinois 60201

Patterned on the Swedish lekoteks begun in Stockholm in 1963, this not-for-profit center specializes in play materials for children with special learning needs. Materials available include infant stimulation toys, puzzles, language development games, science learning aids, and books for parents and children.

National Association for the Education of Young Children
1834 Connecticut Avenue, N.W.
Washington, D.C. 20009

Write for its list of publications; NAEYC also sponsors meetings for professionals in early childhood education.

National Center for Clinical Infant Programs
733 15th Street, N.W.
Suite 912
Washington, D.C. 20005

Publishes a newsletter called *Zero to Three;* sponsors programs and training institutes on infant development.

National Institute of Child Health and Human Development
Office of Research Reporting
Building 31, Room 2A-32
9000 Rockville Pike
Bethesda, Maryland 20205

The government's lead agency for research on the development of young children offers research reports and booklets.

National Institute of Mental Health
Office of Public Information

Appendix: Information, Please: Resources for Parents

Room 15-102
5600 Fishers Lane
Rockville, Maryland 20857

The government's lead agency for research on psychological health offers numerous pamphlets and booklets on the mental health of infants and young children, including an excellent science monograph called "Development of Mental Health in Infancy."

Society for Research in Child Development
University of Chicago
5801 Ellis Avenue
Chicago, Illinois 60637

This is an academic organization that publishes research reports and a quarterly journal, *Child Development*, and sponsors a biennial meeting of professionals in the field of early childhood development.

Selected Bibliography

Research results reported in recent articles in professional journals devoted to child development, medicine, pyschology, and the basic sciences helped to bolster the underlying conclusions presented here. These journals include *Science, The New England Journal of Medicine, American Psychologist, Child Development, Childhood Education,* and *Young Children.* Instead of listing all these articles, we have tried to give complete credit by name to the researchers whose work we have cited throughout this book.

We are indebted to these scientists, many of whom are pioneers who have written extensively of their findings in the professional literature. Some of those mentioned were interviewed in person or by telephone, while others generously shared findings from their work in personal communications.

Several conferences and workshops produced significant contributions. Among them were meetings sponsored by the National Center for Clinical Infant Programs; the American Psychological Association; the Junior League of Washington (D.C.); the National Institute of Child Health and Human Development; the Home and School Institute, Inc.; The Hospital for Sick Children in conjunction with Children's Hospital National Medical Center and the American Medical Women's Association; the Association for Children and Adults with Learning Disabilities; Burton L. White's Center for Parent Education in Newton, Massachusetts; and George Washington University. Harry Wachs, co-author of *Thinking Goes to School,* a book about putting Piaget's theories into practice in the classroom, conducted the workshop at George Washington University.

A Nation at Risk: The Imperative for Educational Reform. National Commission on Excellence in Education, U.S. Department of Education, Washington, D.C., 1983

Adelson, Edna, Shapiro, Vivian, and Bennett, John, "The Training of Community Mental Health Clinicians as Infant Specialists." *Infant Mental Health Journal*, Vol. 3, No. 2 (Summer 1982).

Ader, Robert, "Psychosomatic and Psychoimmunologic Research" (presidential address). *Psychosomatic Medicine*, Vol. 42, No. 3 (May 1980).

Ader, Robert, Cohen, Nicholas, and Grota, Lee J., "Adrenal Involvement in Conditioned Imunosuppression." *International Journal of Immunopharmacology*, Vol. 1 (1979).

Ader, Robert, and Cohen, Nicholas, "Behaviorally Conditioned Immunosuppression." *Psychosomatic Medicine*, Vol. 37, No. 4 (July/August 1975).

Ader, Robert, and Cohen, Nicholas, "Conditioned Immunopharmacologic Responses," in *Psychoneuroimmunology* (New York: Academic Press, 1981).

American Academy of Pediatrics, "Policy Statement." *Pediatrics*, Vol. 70, No. 5 (November 1982).

Anderson, Barry F., *The Complete Thinker*. Englewood Cliffs, N. J.: Prentice-Hall, Inc., 1980.

Beckwith, Leila, and Cohen, Sarale E., "Home Environment and Cognitive Competence in Preterm Children in the First Five Years," in *Home Environment and Early Mental Development* (New York: Academic Press, prepublication excerpt.)

Berman, Phyllis W., "Social Context as a Determinant of Sex Differences in Adults' Attraction to Infants." *Developmental Psychology*, Vol. 12, No. 4 (1976).

Berman, Phyllis W., "Are Women More Responsive Than Men to the Young? A Review of Developmental and Situational Variables." *Psychological Bulletin*, Vol. 88, No. 3 (1980).

Berman, Phyllis W., and Zahn-Waxler, Carolyn, "Children's Nurturance to Younger Children: Age, Sex, and the Situation." Paper presented at the biennial meeting of the Society

Selected Bibliography

for Research in Child Development, Detroit, Michigan, April 1983.

Bettelheim, Bruno, *The Uses of Enchantment*. New York: Vintage Books, 1977.

Bornstein, Marc H., and Marks, Lawrence E., "Color Revisionism." *Psychology Today* (January 1982).

Bradley, L., and Bryant, P. E., "Categorizing Sounds and Learning to Read—a Causal Connection." *Nature*, Vol. 301, No. 5899 (February 1983).

Brazelton, T. Berry, M.D., *Infants and Mothers* (revised edition). A Merloyd Lawrence Book. New York: Dell Publishing Co., Inc., 1983.

Brazelton, T. Berry, M.D., *Toddlers and Parents*. A Delta Book. New York: Dell Publishing Co., Inc., 1974.

Browne, Martha, and Hopson, June, "Making a Mess Creatively: An Art Program for 2-Year-Olds." *Childhood Education* (January/February 1983).

Bruner, Jerome S., *The Process of Education*. New York: Vintage Books, 1963.

Cazenave, Noel A., "Middle-Income Black Fathers: An Analysis of the Provider Role." *The Family Coordinator* (October 1979).

Cesarean Childbirth. U.S. Department of Health and Human Services, Public Health Service, National Institutes of Health. NIH Publication No. 82-2067, October 1981.

Chance, Paul, *Learning Through Play*. Johnson & Johnson Baby Products Company Pediatric Round Table Series. New York: Gardner Press, Inc., 1979.

Chance, Paul, "The Remedial Thinker." *Psychology Today* (October 1981).

Child and Adolescent Development. An Evaluation and Assessment of the State of the Science. National Institute of Child Health and Human Development. Public Health Service, U.S. Department of Health and Human Services, 1980.

Children's Books of the Year, 1983 edition. The Child Study Children's Book Committee at Bank Street College. New York, 1983.

Cohen, Sarale E., Sigman, Marian, Parmelee, Arthur H., and Beckwith, Leila, "Perinatal Risk and Developmental Outcome in Preterm Infants." *Seminars in Perinatology*, Vol. 6, No. 4 (October 1982).

Cohn, Jeffrey F., and Tronick, Edward Z., "Three-Month-Old Infants' Reaction to Simulated Maternal Depression." *Child Development*, Vol. 54 (February 1983).

Collins, Raymond C., "Child Care and the States: The Comparative Licensing Study." *Young Children*, Vol. 38, No. 7 (July 1983).

DeMause, Lloyd, ed., *The History of Childhood*. New York: Harper & Row, Publishers, 1975.

Edwards, Betty, *Drawing on the Right Side of the Brain*. Boston: Houghton Mifflin Co., 1979.

Erikson, Erik H., *Childhood and Society*. New York: W. W. Norton & Company, Inc., 1950.

Esbensen, Steen B., "Where Can Children Play?" *High/Scope Resource*, Vol. 2, No. 1 (1983).

Families Today. Science Monographs (2 volumes). U.S. Department of Health, Education, and Welfare, Public Health Service, Alcohol, Drug Abuse, and Mental Health Adminstration, 1979.

Flynn, James R., "Now the Great American IQ Increase." *Nature*, Vol. 301, No. 24 (February 1983).

Fraiberg, Selma H., "Ghosts in the Nursery: A Psychoanalytic Approach to the Problems of Impaired Infant-Mother Relationships," in *Clinical Studies in Infant Mental Health: The First Year of Life* (New York: Basic Books, 1980).

Fraiberg, Selma H., *The Magic Years*. New York: Charles Scribner's Sons, 1959.

Freud, Sigmund, *A General Introduction to Psychoanalysis*. New York: Washington Square Press, Inc., 1960.

Furth, Hans G., and Wachs, Harry, *Thinking Goes to School: Piaget's Theory in Practice*. New York: Oxford University Press, Inc., 1975.

Gallo, Robert C., Salahuddin, Syed Z., Popovic, Mikulas, et al. "Frequent Detection and Isolation of Cytopathic Retrovi-

Selected Bibliography

ruses (HTLV-III) from Patients with AIDS and at Risk for AIDS." *Science*, Vol. 224, No. 4648 (May 4, 1984).

Gilliam, Kathleen, "Parents' Ambivalence Toward Their Newborn Baby: A Problem in Community and Professional Denial." *Child Welfare*, Vol. LX, No. 7 (July/August 1981).

Greenspan, Stanley I., "Twelve to Eighteen Months: The Stage of the Second Year," excerpted from *Psychopathology and Adaptation in Infancy and Early Childhood: Principles of Clinical Diagnosis and Preventive Intervention* (New York: International Universities Press, 1981).

Grimberg, Salomon, "Putting Art on the Couch." *Vision*, Vol. 4, No. 11 (November 1981).

Henry, James P., and Ely, Daniel L., "Emotional Stress: Physiology." *Primary Cardiology* (August 1979).

Hier, Daniel B., and Crowley, William F., Jr., "Spatial Ability in Androgen-Deficient Men." *The New England Journal of Medicine*, Vol. 306, No. 20 (May 20, 1983).

Honig, Alice Sterling, "Television and Young Children." Research in Review, *Young Children*, Vol. 38, No. 5 (May 1983).

Infancy in the Eighties: Social Policy and the Earliest Years of Life. National Center for Clinical Infant Programs, July 1983.

James, Muriel, and Jongeward, Dorothy, *Born to Win: Transactional Analysis with Gestalt Experiments*. Reading, Massachusetts: Addison-Wesley Publishing Company, 1971.

Jusczyk, Peter W., Pisoni, David B., Reed, Marjorie A., Fernald, Anne, and Myers, Mary, "Infants' Discrimination of the Duration of a Rapid Spectrum Change in Nonspeech Signals." *Science*, Vol. 222, No. 4620 (October 14, 1983).

Keeshan, Bob, "Families and Television." *Young Children*, Vol. 38, No. 3 (March 1983).

Lamb, Michael E., "Paternal Influences and the Father's Role: A Personal Perspective." *American Psychologist*, Vol. 34, No. 10 (October 1979).

MacKinnon, Donald W., "Environments That Favor Creativity." The Henry A. Murray Award Address given at the 1982 annual meeting of the American Psychological Association, Washington, D.C., August 1982.

May, Rollo, *The Courage to Create*. New York: Bantam Books, Inc., 1976.

McGlone, Jeanette, "Sex Differences in Human Brain Asymmetry: A Critical Survey." *The Behavioral and Brain Sciences*, Vol. 3 (1980).

Mill, John Stuart, *The Autobiography of John Stuart Mill*. Garden City, New York: Doubleday & Company, Inc.

Parke, Ross D., "Perspectives on Father–Infant Interaction," in *The Handbook of Infant Development*, edited by Joy D. Osofsky (New York: John Wiley & Sons, Inc., 1979).

Pedersen, Frank A., and Robson, Kenneth S., "Father Participation in Infancy." *American Journal of Orthopsychiatry*, Vol. 39, No. 3 (April 1969).

Pedersen, Frank A., "Mother, Father, and Infant as an Interactive System." Paper presented at the annual meeting of the American Psychological Association, Chicago, Illinois, September 1975.

Pelletier, Kenneth R., *Mind as Healer, Mind as Slayer*. A Delta Book. New York: Dell Publishing Co., Inc., 1977.

Perspectives on Human Deprivation: Biological, Psychological, and Sociological. National Institute of Child Health and Human Development, Public Health Service, U.S. Department of Health, Education, and Welfare (now the U.S. Department of Health and Human Services), 1968.

Piaget, Jean, *The Language and Thought of the Child*. Meridian Books. Cleveland: The World Publishing Company, 1955.

Piaget, Jean, *The Psychology of Intelligence*. Totowa, New Jersey: Littlefield, Adams & Co., 1976.

Pitcher, Evelyn Goodenough, and Prelinger, Ernst, *Children Tell Stories: An Analysis of Fantasy*. New York: International Universities Press, Inc., 1963.

Read, Merrill S., *Malnutrition, Learning, and Behavior*. National Institute of Child Health and Human Development. Center for Research for Mothers and Children. DHEW publication No. (NIH) 76-1036, April 1976.

Report of the Research Briefing Panel on Neuroscience. Committee on Science, Engineering, and Public Policy. National Academy of Sciences, National Academy of Engineering,

Selected Bibliography

Institute of Medicine. National Academy Press, Washington, D.C., 1983.

Review of Head Start Research Since 1970, A. U.S. Department of Health and Human Services, Administration for Children, Youth and Families, Head Start Bureau, 1983.

Rosenfeld, Anne H., and Rosenfeld, Sam A., *The Roots of Individuality: Brain Waves and Perception.* An NIMH Program Report. Alcohol, Drug Abuse, and Mental Health Administration. Public Health Service, U.S. Department of Health, Education, and Welfare, 1976. Reprinted 1978.

Sagan, Carl, *The Dragons of Eden: Speculations on the Evolution of Human Intelligence.* New York: Ballantine Books, 1977.

Schweinhart, Lawrence J., and Weikart, David P., *Young Children Grow Up: The Effects of the Perry Preschool Program on Youths through Age 15.* Ypsilanti, Michigan: High/Scope Educational Research Foundation, 1980.

Selye, Hans, "Stress and the Reduction of Distress." *Primary Cardiology* (August 1979).

Selye, Hans, *Stress without Distress.* A Signet Book. New York: New American Library, 1974.

"Social/Behavioral Effects of Violence on Television." Hearing Before the Subcommittee on Telecommunications, Consumer Protection, and Finance, of the Committee on Energy and Commerce, U.S. House of Representatives, 97th Congress. October 21, 1981. Serial No. 97-84. U.S. Government Printing Office, Washington, D.C., 1982.

Starkey, Prentice, Spelke, Elizabeth, and Gelman, Rochel, "Detection of Intermodal Numerical Correspondence by Human Infants." *Science*, Vol. 222, No. 4620 (October 14, 1983).

Stenberg, Craig R., Campos, Joseph J., and Emde, Robert N., "The Facial Expression of Anger in Seven-Month-Old Infants." *Child Development*, Vol. 54 (February 1983).

Stern, Daniel N., Jaffe, Joseph, Beebe, Beatrice, and Bennett, Stephen L., "Vocalizing in Unison and in Alternation: Two Modes of Communication Within the Mother-Infant Dyad." *Annals of the New York Academy of Sciences. Developmental Psycholinguistics and Communication Disorders*, Vol. 263 (1975).

Sternberg, Robert J., and Davidson, Janet E., "The Mind of the Puzzler." *Psychololgy Today* (June 1982).

Sternberg, Robert J., "Who's Intelligent?" *Psychology Today* (April 1982).

"Stress and Immunity." In *Focus*, a publication of Harvard University's News Office for the Medical Area (April 22, 1982).

Stroebel, Charles F., "Voluntary Self-Regulation of Stress," in *Inner Balance: The Power of Holistic Healing* (Englewood Cliffs, New Jersey: Prentice-Hall, Inc., 1979.)

Suzuki, Shinichi, *Nurtured By Love: A New Approach to Education*. Smithtown, New York: Exposition Press, 1969.

Thelen, Esther, and Fisher, Donna M., "From Spontaneous to Instrumental Behavior: Kinematic Analysis of Movement Changes During Very Early Learning." *Child Development*, Vol. 54 (1983).

Vaillant, George E., "Natural History of Male Psychologic Health." *The New England Journal of Medicine*, Vol. 301, No. 23 (December 6, 1979).

Weissbourd, Bernice, and Musick, Judith, eds., *Infants: Their Social Environments*. National Association for the Education of Young Children, Washington, D.C., 1981.

Whimbey, Arthur, and Whimbey, Linda Shaw, *Intelligence Can Be Taught*. New York: E. P. Dutton, 1980.

White, Burton L., *The First Three Years of Life*. New York: Avon Books, 1975.

Zigler, Edward, and Berman, Winnie, "Discerning the Future of Early Childhood Intervention." *American Psychologist*, Vol. 38, No. 8 (August 1983).

Index

Abstract-reasoning approach to reading, 80, 81
Abstract thinking, 61
Acquired immune deficiency syndrome (AIDS), 182
ACT (Action for Children's Television), 171, 172
Action toys, 112
Active learning, inactive learning and, 44–45
Adams, Russell, J., 69
Adapted child, 109
Ader, Robert, 187–188, 189
Administration for Children, Youth, and Families, 245
Adrenal glands, 184
Adrenaline, 185, 189, 199
Adult thinking, child thinking and, 45–46, 61
Agoraphobia, 209
Alliteration, 79–80
Alphabet books, 133
Altman, Joseph, 57
Altruism, storytelling and, 137
American Academy of Pediatrics (AAP), 30–31
American Federation of Government Employees (AFGE), 232–233
American Psychological Association, 265
American Psychologist, 219, 265
American Speech-Language-Hearing Association, 73, 167
Analytical education, 49–50
Anger, 51, 165
Angus and the Cat (Flack), 136–137, 148
Antibiotics, 77

Antibodies, 182–183, 184
coached behavior and, 187, 188–189
Antigens, 182
Antihistamine drugs, 77
Association of Junior Leagues, 267
At-risk children, special help for, 25
Axons, 53

Babies (newborns)
language and, 78
whole-body learning and, 85–86
Baby carriers, 96–97
Baby talk, fallacy of, 75
Bacteria, 182
Bank Street College of Education, 133, 145
Barcus, R. Earle, 171
Barnard, Kathryn M., 25
Bathing, planned stimulation and, 91, 95
Batman, 168
Behavior
coached, 187, 188–189
goal-oriented, 152
with other people, guidelines for, 38
rational-emotive approach to, 164–165
Berman, Phyllis W., 220, 265
Berne, Eric, 109, 115, 141
Bettelheim, Bruno, 131, 132, 133, 142, 143
Better Baby Institute, 30
Biofeedback, blood pressure and, 215
Biology, preschoolers and, 258
Birth process, fathers and, 221–223
Bleeding ulcers, 185
Blocks, 107
Blood pressure, biofeedback and, 215

Index

Body exploration, *see* Whole-body learning
Body language, storytelling and, 132
Bohannon, Paul, 228
Bonding, 23–26
  fathers and, 24, 220–221
Books, 35, 163
  picture books, 72, 100–101
  for preschoolers, 133–134, 145–148
  reading readiness and, 143–145
Born to Win (James and Jongeward), 109
Borysenko, Joan, 191–192
Bowlby, John, 23
Bradley, Lynette, 79–80, 81
Brain, 51–52
  biology and function of, 55–56, 59–60
  color recognition and, 68–69
  creativity and, 153
  the ears as learning tool, 73–77
  eye/hand coordination and, 72–73
  the eyes as learning tool, 70–73
  growth of, 57–58
  immune system and, 59–60, 186, 187–190
  numerical awareness and, 67–68
  placebo effect and, 212–213
  stimulation and, 56–57, 59–60
  working of, 53–56
Brazelton, T. Berry, 26, 89
Breznitz, Shlomo, 193
Bronfenbrenner, Urie, 111–112
Bronstein, Marc H., 68
Browne, Martha, 162, 163
Bruner, Jerome S., 237, 257
Bryant, Peter E., 79–80, 81

Cabbage Patch dolls, 123
Cancer, 190
  depression and, 186, 190
  stress and, 191–192
Cannon, Walter, 185
Catecholamines, 185, 189
Cause-and-effect toys, 21, 114–115, 117
CDA National Credentialing Program, 246
Center for Parent Education, 238, 267
Cerebral cortex, 53, 56

Cesarean sections, fathers and, 222–223
Child advocates, working mothers and, 238–239
Childbirth education classes, 229
Child-care centers, *see* Preschools
Child-care leave, 232–233
Child-care licensing requirements in U.S., 245–246
Child Development, 271
Child development associate (CDA) credentials, 245, 246
Child development research, 27–29, 247–248
Child Health and Human Development, 223
Children's Hospital National Medical Center, 241
"Child's Garden of Verses, A" (Stevenson), 107
Child Study Children's Book Committee, 133, 145, 147
Child thinking, adult thinking and, 45–46, 61
Chuckie (Weiss), 133, 146
Church-affiliated child-care centers, 246
Clean Enough (Henkes), 134, 146
Coactional vocalizing, 111
Cohen, Nicholas, 187
Cohen, Sarale, 93–94
Collins, Raymond C., 245, 246
Coloring books, 163
Colors
  matching of, 161, 175
  playrooms and, 120
  recognition of, 68–69
Coltheart, Max, 80
Completion, play and, 108
Computers
  the brain and, 54
  writing-to-read system and, 84–85
Concrete operations stage of child development, 22
Conjugate gaze, 70, 71
Conscience, developing, 141
Consider-the-consequences thinking, 202
Construction paper, 162, 163
Contingency concept, 166–167

Index

Control, 197–215
  ICPS and, 201–206, 215
  kiddie QR and, 198–201, 206, 215
  learned helplessness and, 206–208
  pain tolerance and, 211–212
  phobias and, 208–210
  placebo effect and, 212–215
Corpus callosum, 54
Cortex, 189
Corticosteroids, 184
Council for National Corporation in Aquatics, Inc., 97, 268
Courage to Create, The (May), 151
Crayons, eye/hand coordination and, 73
Creativity (creative learning), 45–46, 151–175
  art materials for, 162–164
  discipline and, 164–167
  home as a learning center, 157–162
  natural opportunities in, 174–175
  nonlinear thinking and, 153–154
  preschools and, 258–259, 261–264
  television and, 167–174
Crowley, William F., Jr., 55
Crying, 165, 166
Csikszentmihalyi, Mihaly, 108
Cultural conditioning, phobias and, 209–210
Cutout patterns, 163
Cyclophosphamide, 188

Day-care centers, *see* Preschools
Decongestant drugs, 77
Delacato, C.H., 30
De Mause, Lloyd, 20, 219–220
Dendrites, 58
Denko, Charles W., 213
Depression, 25, 50–51
  coping with, 192–194
  immune system and, 191
  steroids and, 186, 190
Descartes, René, 179, 180–181
Developmental classrooms, 259
"Development of Mental Health in Infancy," 271
Development styles, 89–90
De Vincentis, Sarah, 121–122
Diapering, planned stimulation and, 91, 95

Discipline, 164–167
Discourse on Method (Descartes), 179
Discovery Toys, 123–124
Dishwashers, unloading, 159
Dollhouses, 108
Doman, Glenn, 30
Doman-Delacato treatment method for child development, 30–31
Dragons of Eden, The (Sagan), 43
Dusting, 13

Ear infections, 76–77
Ears, 65–66, 73–77
  use of, guidelines for, 37–38
Education, high school, quality of, 248–250
Educational television channels, 171
Educational toy lending libraries, 121–122
Educational toys, 56, 121–124
  eye/hand coordination and, 73
  homemade, 126–127
Egan, James H., 241
Egocentricity, 61, 115, 136, 137, 258
Ellis, Albert, 164
Emotional growth, 48–51
Emotions, 164, 165, 189–190, 191–192
  early detection of problems, 26
Empathy, storytelling and, 137
Endorphins, 213
Environment, creativity and, 155–157
Esbensen, Steen B., 121
European toys, 122, 123, 124
Exhaustion response, 186, 190
Expectation principle, 207
Exploration, *see* Whole-body learning
Eye/hand coordination, 72–73
Eyes, 24, 65–66, 70–73
  use of, guidelines for, 37

Failure-to-thrive syndrome, 23, 197
Fairy tales, 131, 132, 142
Family Focus/Family Resource Coalition, 268
Family room as learning center, 160–161, 174–175
Fantasy, 142–143
  creativity and, 151
"Fatherhood: The Pleasures and Pains" (educational course), 229

283

Index

"Fatherhood After the Break: Parenting Alone" (educational course), 229
Fathers (fathering), 219–233
  birthing process and, 221–223
  bonding and, 24, 220–221
  child's concept of, 66
  fostering fatherhood, 229–230
  infant signals and, 223–224
  infant stimulation and, 224–227
  paternity leave and, 231–233
  play styles of, 120, 225–226, 227, 232
  as single parents, 227, 228–229
Fear, 189–190
Federal Communications Commission (FCC), 171
Feeding, planned stimulation and, 91, 95
Feelings, *see* Emotional growth
Female brain, male brain and, 54–56
Female hormones, 55
Feuerstein, Reuven, 255, 256
Fields, Mary Jane, 117, 118
Fight-or-flight response, 185–186, 189
  kiddie QR and, 198–199
Finger painting, 102, 103
Firstborn, fathers and, 226–227
Fisher, Donna M., 95, 96
Flack, Marjorie, 148
Flash cards, 28, 29, 35, 36
  fallacy of, 43–44, 46, 47, 58, 259
Flexiplace, 242
Flextime workers, 230
Flow, 108
Focusing (eyes), 24, 70–71
Food coloring, 162
Formal operations stage of child development, 22
Fraiberg, Selma H., 19
Free association, 61
  storytelling and, 142–143
Freud, Sigmund, 20, 61
  preschool thinking and, 61
Friedrich, Lynette, 168
Frodi, Ann M., 223
Fungi, 182
Furth, Hans G., 260

Gallo, Robert C., 182
Games, 56, 99, 102, 112

Gamma globulins, 182–183
Gazing as prespeech form of communication, 158
Gelman, Rochel, 67
Gilliam, Kathleen, 25
Girls, phobias and, 208–210
Glia, 58
Goal-oriented behavior, 152
Going with the flow, 108
Greenspan, Stanley I., 26, 93, 99, 100, 101, 102, 103
Growth readiness, 29–30
Guilt, 141

Handelmann, Gail E., 52
Hands, use of, guidelines for, 37
Harlow, Harry, 22–23
"Harvard at one" syndrome, 29
Harvard University, 113, 170
Hawkins, Pamela, 85
Head Start, 248, 264–265, 268
Healing, 180–181
  power of suggestion and, 212–215
  steroids and, 185
Hearing, 73–77
  development of, 65
  ear infections and, 76–77
  music and, 24
Hearing specialists, 76–77
Heart attack, 185
Hello Kitty Sleeps Over (Harris), 134, 146
Helplessness, 186, 190
  See also Learned helplessness
Hemispheres of the brain, 53, 54
Henkes, Kevin, 146
Hier, Daniel B., 55
High school education, quality of, in U.S., 248–250
High/Scope Educational Research Foundation, 262, 269
High/Scope Resource, 269
Hippocrates, 155
History of Childhood, The (deMause), 20, 220
Holistic health movement, 215
Holland, Margaret, 198, 200–201
Home and School Institute, 157, 269
Homemade educational toys, 126–127
Honig, Alice S., 167, 168, 169, 170

284

Index

Hopson, June, 162, 163
Hormones, 184
   male and female, 55
Horton, Paul C., 119
Hospitals
   bonding and, 24–26
   infant stimulation program and, 24–26
Household chores, creativity and, 113, 161–162
Househusband, 219, 229
Houseplants, 161
Housewife's disease, 209
Howell, Mary C., 239–240
HTLV-III virus, 182
Huggable toys, 119
Human Learning and Behavior Branch of the National Institute of Child Health and Human Development, 220
Hyperactivity, 25
Hypothalamus, 189

IBM Corporation, 83, 84, 85
Illiteracy in the U.S., 249
Images
   creativity and, 154
   language of, 131, 133
   visual perception and, 72
Immune-conditioning theory, 188–189
Immune system, 181–182
   the brain and, 59–60, 186, 187–190
   catecholamines and, 185
   depression and, 191
   emotions and, 189–190, 191–192
   steroids and, 185, 186
   stress and, 190, 192, 206
Inactive learning, active learning and, 44–45
Independence, 101–103, 191
Infants, 24–26
   art materials for, 93, 163–164
   moral sense of, 140–141
   reading readiness for, 144
   responsive caregiving for, 93–95
   storytelling and, 131, 132, 133
   See also Preschoolers
Infant signals, 223–224
Infant stimulation, *see* Stimulation (planned stimulation)

Infant Stimulation Education Association, 25, 269
Initiative, 191
Institute of Living, 198, 200
Institutes for the Achievement of Human Potential, 30, 31
Intellectual development, stages of, 21–22, 61, 167–168, 257
Intensity of awareness, 153–154
Interpersonal cognitive problem-solving (ICPS), 201–206, 215
IPD News, 85

Jack-in-the-boxes, 114–115
James, Muriel, 109
Job sharing, 230
Jongeward, Dorothy, 109
Jungle gyms, 102

Kandel, Eric, 52
Keeshan, Bob, 172–173
Kennell, John, 23–24
Kicking exercises, 95–96
Kick patterns, 95–96
Kiddie QR, 198–201, 206, 215
Kindergarten, 243
King, Robert, 137, 141
Kirk, Samuel A., 46
Kitchen as learning center, 157–158, 159–160, 174
Klaus, Marshall, 23–24
Krasnegor, Norman A., 78
Krogh, Suzanne Lowell, 136

Lamb, Michael, 219, 223, 227, 231–232
Lamme, Linda Leonard, 136
Language
   of images, 131, 133
   learning to talk, 77–79
   seven major steps in, 73–75
   talking to children, 79–82, 92, 101
   vocabulary skills, 75–76
   writing-to-read system and, 83–85
Language and Thought of the Child, The (Piaget), 20
Larm, Elizabeth, 121
Larynx, 77
Laundry room as learning center, 113, 158, 161, 175

Index

Learned helplessness, 194, 197, 206–208
Learning disabilities, 46–47
Learning society, 257
Left side of the brain, 53
Lekoteks, 121–122, 269–270
Lennon, John, 219
Lennon, Sean, 219
Leukemia, 184
Light switches, turning on, 160, 175
Limbic system of the brain, fear and, 189–190
Linear thinking, 61, 152, 153
Listening, 73–75
Living room as learning center, 160–161
Loss-of-control response, 186
Ludington, Susan M., 25, 91, 269
Lumpkin, Bettejane, 233
Lustig, Robert S., 25

McCuaig, Susannah M., 82
McEnroe, John, 34
MacKinnon, Donald W., 155, 156
McMaster University, 68–69
McNichol, Kristy, 47
Magic Years, The (Fraiberg), 19
Male brain, female brain and, 54–56
Male hormones, 55
Male support groups, 230
Malnutrition, growth of the brain and, 58
Martin, John Henry, 83–85
Massachusetts, University of, 51
Mass-produced toys, 122–123
Maternal antibodies, 182–183
Maurer, Daphne, 69
May, Rollo, 151, 153–154, 155
Means-end thinking, 202
Mediated learning, 255–256
Meditation, 198
Mental health, illness and, 180, 190–191
Middle ear infection, 76–77
Mill, James, 49
Mill, John Stuart, 49–50
Mind/body connection, 179–183
Minnesota Early Learning Design (MELD), 268
Misbehavior, placebo effect and, 214

Mister Rogers' Neighborhood, 168
Mixing bowls, 116–117, 126
Mobiles, 107, 116, 158–159
Monoamine oxidase (MAO) inhibitors, 209
Mood-lifting trips, 193
Moral growth, storytelling and, 140–142, 143
Morality of constraint, 140
More, Ann, 96
More, Michael, 96
Mothers (mothering), 220–221
 child's concept of, 66
 infant signals and, 223–224
 infant stimulation and, 224–226
 play styles of, 120, 225–226, 227, 232
 scientific studies on importance of, 22–24
 working, child development and, 238–242
Mother-tongue approach to learning, 32–34
Muscle knowledge, 96
Music, 24
 mother-tongue approach to, 32–34

National Association for the Education of Young Children (NAEYC), 144, 172, 247, 252, 270
National Center for Clinical Infant Programs, 26, 270
National Coalition on Television Violence (NCTV), 173
National Commission on Excellence in Education, 248–249, 255, 256–257
National Day Care Study (1979), 243–244
National Institute of Child Health and Human Development, 57, 78, 270
National Institute of Mental Health (NIMH), 26, 52, 137, 173, 201, 205, 209, 270–271
Nation at Risk, A (report on U.S. high school education), 249–250
Natural learning, 44–45, 48, 66
Natural stimulation, 34–35
Nature, 80
Nemeth, Lane, 123–124

Index

Nerve cells, 54, 57–60
Nerve fibers, 53
Nerve impulses, 53
Nervous system
 the brain and, 51
 testosterone and, 55
 trial-and-error learning and, 47
Neuroblasts, 57, 59
Neurons, 52, 58
Neuroscience, 51–52
Neurotransmitters, 51–52, 53, 59, 60
New England Journal of Medicine, The, 55, 189
Nightmares, 193
Nonlinear thinking, 153–154
Notes to Myself (Prather), 65
Nouns, learning language and, 75
Numerical awareness, 67–68
Nurses
 bonding and, 24–25
 disease prevention and, 183
Nurture by Love (Suzuki), 89
Nutritious food, growth of the brain and, 58

Object permanence, 115, 153
O'Donahue, Thomas, 52
Opiate drugs, 213
Optional thinking, 202
Otitis media, 76–77
Outdoor playrooms, 120–121, 252

Pacifiers, 107
Pain
 threshold of, 211
 tolerance for, 211–212
Panic, 194
 agoraphobia and, 209
Pans, 116
Parental Insurance Plans, 231
Parents Without Partners, 230
Park Bench (play group), 229
Parke, Ross D., 223, 224, 225, 226
Passivity, 186, 194
Paternity leave, 231–233
Patterns, cutout, 163
Pavlov, Ivan, 187
Peabody Picture Vocabulary Test (PPVT), 243–244

Pedersen, Frank A., 223
Pediatrics, 30
Perry Preschool Program, 261–264, 265
Personality, planned stimulation and, 90
Phobia clinics, 209
Phobias, 208–210
Phonetic approach to reading, 80–82
Phonological awareness, 79–80
Physical contact as planned stimulation, 91–92, 95, 96
Physical readiness for learning, 260
Piaget, Jean, 20, 115, 140, 153, 167, 174, 256
 preschools and, 259–261
 stages of child's intellectual development and, 21, 61, 167–168, 257
Picture books, 100–101
 visual perception and, 72
Pitcher, Evelyn Goodenough, 138, 139, 140
Pituitary gland, 189
Placebo effect, 212–215
Plato, 49
Play, 107–127
 as builder of competence, 107–109
 educational toys for, 121–124, 126–127
 household chores as, 113
 parents and, 112–117, 124–126
  play styles, 120–121, 225–226, 227, 232
 puppets, 117–119, 126, 127
 toy selection, 113–117
 vocalizing in unison, 111
Play-Doh, 162
Playrooms, 120–121, 252
Play styles, mother/father differences in, 120–121, 225–226, 227, 232
Postpartum Project, 25–26
Pots, 116
Power of suggestion as healing force, 212–215
Prather, Hugh, 65
Precocity, 46–48
Preconversation (talking back), 94, 99–100
Prelinger, Ernst, 138, 140
Premature babies, 24, 36

287

Index

Pre-operational stage of child development, 21–22, 61, 167–168
  learning experiences for, 257–258
Prerational thinking, 61
Preschoolers
  ICPS skills and, 202–206
  reading readiness for, 144–145
  recommended books for, 133–134, 145–148
  storytelling by, 137–140
Preschool Inventory (PSI), 243, 244
Preschools, 243–247
  creativity and, 258–259, 261–264
  guide to selection of, 240–242, 250–252
  Piaget's teachings and, 259–261
  quality of, 248
  taxes for, 248
Preschool teachers, 247–248
Priest, Louise, 97
Primary Intervention Program (PIP), 25
Primary process thinking, 61
Process of Education, The (Bruner), 237, 257
"Professional Woman as Mother, The," 240
Psychoneuroimmunology, 181–182, 187–188, 192, 194
Puppets, 117–119
  homemade, 126–127
  learning ICPS skills with, 203–204
Puzzles, 56, 112

Quieting reflex (QR), 198–201

Radecki, Thomas, 173
Radke-Yarrow, Martin, 137, 141
Rational-emotive approach to behavior, 164–165
Read, Merrill S., 57
Reading, 35
  recommended books for preschoolers, 133–134, 145–148
  talking to children and, 79–82
  writing-to-read system and, 83–85
Reading readiness, 143–145
Real learning, 28–29
Relaxation, stress control and, 198–201
Remedial education courses, 250

Resiliency, 190–194, 198
Responsive caregiving, 93–95
Rhyme, 79–80
Rich, Dorothy, 157, 159
Right side of the brain, 53
Rote learning, 29

Sadness, coping with, 192–194
Sagan, Carl, 43
Scholastic Aptitude Tests (SAT), decline in scores on (1963–1980), 249
Schweinhart, Lawrence J., 262, 263
Sechenov, Ivan M., 34
Security blankets, 119
Selye, Hans, 183–184, 197, 198
Senses, 65–86
  color recognition and, 68–69
  hearing, 73–77
  learning to talk, 77–79
    seven major steps in, 73–75
    talking to children, 79–82, 92, 101
  numerical awareness and, 67–68
  vision, 70–73
  writing-to-read system and, 83–85
Sensorimotor experiences, 66
Sensory stimulation, 34–35
Sequential thinking, 61
Serotonin, 52
Sesame Street, 170
Sharing, storytelling and, 136–137
Shure, Myrna B., 201, 202, 203, 205
Silverman, Morton, 98
Single-parent families, 227, 228–229
Sleep/waking cycles, chart for recording, 38–40
Socialized thinking, 61
Society for Research in Child Development, 27, 271
Speaking skills
  hearing and, 73–75
  learning to talk, 77–79
    seven major steps in, 73–75
    talking to children, 79–82, 92, 101
Spelke, Elizabeth S., 67
Spelling, talking to children and, 80–82
Spier, Peter, 147
Spitz, René, 23

Index

Spivack, George, 201, 202, 203, 205
Spock, Benjamin, 43–44, 46
Starkey, Prentice, 67
Stein, Aletha, 168
Stern, Daniel N., 111, 158
Steroids, 184–185
   loss-of-control response and, 186, 190
Stevenson, Robert Louis, 107
Stimulation (planned stimulation), 25, 34–35, 89–103, 224–227
   brain development and, 56–57, 59–60
   infants and, 24–26
   learning and, 44–45
   moods and, 97–98, 100, 103
   responding to, 38–40
   responsive caregiving and, 93–95
   toddlers and, 98–101
Stoebel, Charles F., 198, 200
Storyboards, 134–135, 137, 140
Storytelling, 131–148
   learning to share and, 136–137
   moral growth and, 140–142, 143
   by preschoolers, 137–140
   puppets and, 117
   reading readiness and, 143–145
   recommended books for preschoolers, 133–134, 145–148
   sense of fantasy and, 142–143
   storyboards, 134, 135, 137, 140
Straight thinking, 201–206
Stress, 183–186
   cancer and, 191–192
   control and, 198
   immune system and, 184, 192, 206
   placebo effect and, 213, 215
   toys and, 197
Stress of Life, The (Selye), 183–184, 185
Stress Without Distress (Selye), 197
Stuffed animals, 119
Superman, 168
Suzuki, Shinichi, 32–33, 35, 89
Sweden
   educational toy lending libraries in, 121
   paternity leave in, 231–232
Swedish Lekotek Association, 121
Swimming classes, 97
Synapse, 53, 58

Talent Education Institute, 32, 33
Talking to children, 79–82, 92, 101
Taxes, preschool education and, 248
Telephones, 160–161, 174
Television, 167–174
   toy-industry advertising on, 122–123
Testosterone, 55
Thelen, Esther, 95, 96
Thinking Goes to School (Furth and Wachs), 260
Timeless thinking, 61
Toddlers, 98–101
   independence and, 101–103
   reading readiness for, 144–145
   storytelling and, 131, 132, 133
   whole-body learning and, 86
   See also Preschoolers
Toes, playing with, 107
Touching, 66, 82
Toy lending libraries, 121–122
Toys, 21, 24, 107–108
   educational, 56, 121–124
   eye/hand coordination and, 73
   homemade, 126–127
   mass-produced, 122–123
   selection of, 112–117, 119
   stress-producing, 197
Toy telephones, 160–161
   preconversations and, 99–100
Tracking (eyes), 70, 71
   planned stimulation and, 92
Transactional analysis, 109
Trial-and-error learning, 47–48, 66
Tricyclic antidepressants, 209
Trust, 191
20/20 vision, 70–71
Typewriting, 83–84

United States (U.S.)
   child-care licensing requirements in, 245–246
   illiteracy in, 249
   quality of high school education in, 248–250
   toy industry in, 122–123
Uses of Enchantment, The (Bettelheim), 131

Vaillant, George E., 190–191
Verbs, learning language and, 75–76

Index

Violence on television, 167–168, 173
Viruses, 182
Vision, 70–73
  development of, 66
Vocabulary
  hearing and, 74–75
  talking to children and, 101
Vocal cords, 77
Vocalizing in unison, 158
  as play, 111
Voice, use of, guidelines for, 37–38

Wachs, Harry, 260
Walking, kick patterns and, 95–96
Weikart, David P., 261–262, 263, 269
Weiss, Nicki, 146
White, Burton L., 26, 79, 113, 158, 238, 267
White blood cells, 182, 184, 185

Whole-body learning, 44–45, 47, 85–86, 259–260
  natural learning and, 44–45, 48, 66
  play as, 107
Whole-body movements, development of, guidelines for, 36–37
Wolfe, Barry, 209, 210
Wood, Benjamin, 83
Wooden spoons, 116, 126–127
Working mothers, child development and, 238–242
Writing-to-read system, 83–85

Yoga, 198

Zahn-Waxler, Carolyn, 137, 141
Zero to Three (newsletter), 270
Zigler, Edward, 265